GILGO BEACH
MURDERS
UNMASKED

*Unveiling Darkness - The Investigation
and Capture of Rex Heuermann.*

Second Edition.

James D. Daley

GILGO BEACH MURDERS UNMASKED

Disclaimer:

Gilgo Beach Murders Unmasked: Unveiling Darkness - The Investigation and Capture of Rex Heuermann is a book that seeks to provide an overview of the Gilgo Beach murder investigation and the subsequent capture of Rex Heuermann. The information presented in this book is based on publicly available sources, official statements, court records, and news reports up till date.

While every effort has been made to ensure accuracy and objectivity, the nature of criminal investigations and legal proceedings involves complexities, uncertainties, and evolving information. The publisher acknowledges the dynamic nature of ongoing events and recognize that new details or developments may come up.

Readers are encouraged to cross-reference the information presented in this book with reliable and up-to-date sources for the latest developments in the Gilgo Beach murder case. This book is not intended to provide legal advice or investigative conclusions but aims to offer a comprehensive narrative of the known facts surrounding the case.

The views, opinions, and interpretations expressed in this book are those of the author and do not necessarily reflect the official stance of law enforcement agencies, legal authorities, or other involved parties.

The names and identifying details of individuals mentioned in this book have been used responsibly and respectfully, considering the sensitivity of the subject matter.

Readers should be aware that true crime narratives may contain disturbing content related to criminal activities and are advised to exercise discretion and sensitivity while engaging with the material. The publisher disclaims any responsibility for the consequences of the reader's interpretation or use of the information provided in this book.

This disclaimer is subject to change as new information becomes available, and the publisher reserve the right to update or amend it accordingly.

Table of Contents

INTRODUCTION

In the idyllic landscape of Long Island's Gilgo Beach, where the gentle lull of waves against the shore was once the only melody, a chilling mystery unfolded, leaving a community in terror and investigators grappling with an unsolved enigma. The Gilgo Beach Murders, a string of gruesome killings, would grip the nation's attention and baffle law enforcement for over a decade.

It all began innocently in December 2010 when a 911 call, tinged with fear and desperation, led police to the desolate shoreline. Shannan Gilbert, a 24-year-old sex worker, had vanished after visiting a client in Oak Park, leaving behind a trail of unanswered questions. The search for Shannan took a dark turn when, instead of her, the remains of 24-year-old Melissa Barthelemy were discovered along Ocean Parkway.

The eerie revelation marked the beginning of a sinister chapter, revealing a clandestine graveyard of bodies meticulously hidden along the beach. The haunting discovery, unfolding over the next year, would uncover the skeletal remains of 11 victims – primarily female escorts, each with their own tragic tale. The sandy shores of Gilgo Beach had unwittingly become the stage for a heinous series of crimes.

As investigators delved into the lives of the victims, a haunting pattern emerged. Many of the women were sex workers, offering their services on platforms like Craigslist. The first four victims, collectively known as "the Gilgo Four" – Melissa Barthelemy, Maureen Brainard-Barnes, Megan Waterman, and Amber Lynn

Costello – were all connected through their involvement in the sex trade. The chilling proximity of their remains raised the specter of a serial killer haunting the shoreline.

Two more victims, Jessica Taylor and Valerie Mack, added to the grim tally. Their lives, cut short in the pursuit of a dark desire, begged for justice. However, the identity of the perpetrator remained elusive, shrouded in the secrets of the Long Island night.

The Mysterious Caller and Shannan Gilbert's Haunting Echo:

As the investigation deepened, Shannan Gilbert's case took on a peculiar resonance. Her 911 call, made in the throes of fear, hinted at a presence that went beyond a mere coincidence. The mysterious caller, alluded to in the call, became a spectral figure in the narrative – an entity that seemed to have a hand in the unfolding tragedy.

Gilbert's disappearance in 2010 triggered a desperate search that inadvertently unraveled the broader mystery. While Shannan's remains were eventually found, her connection to the other victims raised unsettling questions. Was there a method to this madness, or was it a cruel twist of fate that brought these lives together on the shores of Gilgo Beach?

Despite the intensity of the investigations, the Gilgo Beach Murders remained an unsolved riddle, shrouded in the fog of uncertainty. The victims' families, haunted by the absence of closure, clamored for justice that seemed elusive. The diverse cast of victims, each with their unique stories, became symbols of a tragedy that transcended individual fates, morphing into a collective wound etched into the community's psyche.

11 | Gilgo Beach Murders Unmasked

The media frenzy surrounding the Gilgo Beach Murders reached its zenith, with documentaries and podcasts attempting to piece together the puzzle. The sinister allure of an unsolved mystery drew the attention of armchair detectives and true crime enthusiasts, all eager to dissect the enigma.

The case might have lingered in the annals of unsolved crimes if not for the awakening of a sleeping giant – a multi-agency task force formed in 2022, determined to unravel the mystery that had haunted Long Island for over a decade. The task force, comprising the FBI, state, and local police departments, injected new life into the investigation.

The Emergence of Rex Heuermann:

In a dramatic turn of events, a potential breakthrough emerged as investigators focused on Rex Heuermann, a seemingly ordinary man living in Massapequa Park, just across the bay from the crime scenes. Heuermann, a registered architect with over 30 years' experience, was about to become a central figure in the Gilgo Beach Murders saga.

The link connecting Heuermann to the crime scenes came in the form of a pickup truck. A witness had reported seeing this truck around the time one of the victims disappeared in 2010. The revelation catapulted Heuermann into the spotlight, transforming the unassuming architect into a prime suspect.

As investigators zeroed in on Heuermann, a cinematic twist unfolded in the form of a discarded pizza box. In an unexpected turn of events, DNA evidence was found on a pizza crust inside the box, a crucial piece of the puzzle that linked Heuermann to the crime scenes. The once-dismissed hair found on one of the victims was now a damning connection, a strand of evidence leading straight to the suspected killer.

The arrest of Rex Heuermann on July 13, 2023, sent shockwaves through the community. The unassuming family man, living just a stone's throw away from the scenes of horror, was now accused of being the elusive Gilgo Beach serial killer. The courtroom drama that unfolded, with Heuermann's not guilty plea and the subsequent legal proceedings, rivaled the tension of a crime thriller.

As the layers of Rex Heuermann's life were peeled back, a disturbing portrait of the accused killer emerged. Obsessive internet searches about the Gilgo Beach killings, sadistic materials, and a penchant for sexually exploitative images of children painted a chilling picture of the man behind the curtain.

The capture of Rex Heuermann marked a triumph for the multi-agency task force and the persistent investigators who refused to let the case fade into obscurity. Suffolk County Police Commissioner Rodney Harrison hailed the arrest, declaring Heuermann a "demon that walks among us."

The arrest brought mixed emotions to the Gilgo Beach community. Relief, for the fiend allegedly responsible for years of terror, was tempered by the realization that darkness had lurked so close to home. The impact on victims' families, who had endured years of uncertainty, was immeasurable.

The Gilgo Beach Murders, now unmasked, left an indelible mark on the collective consciousness. The legacy of darkness, etched into the sandy shores and the memories of those touched by the tragedy, became

15 | **Gilgo Beach Murders Unmasked**

a somber reminder of the fragility of safety in seemingly peaceful havens.

The tale of the Gilgo Beach Murders, with its twists and turns, unfolds as a narrative that transcends the boundaries of true crime. It's a story of lives cut short, families shattered, and a community forever changed. As Rex Heuermann awaits his fate in the courtroom, the shadows that once enveloped Gilgo Beach are slowly dissipating, unveiling a semblance of justice for the victims and their grieving families.

Investigation into the Gilgo Beach Murders: Unveiling Darkness (2010-2024)

The investigation into the Gilgo Beach Murders unfolded as a gripping tale of mystery, horror, and justice, leaving an indelible mark on Long Island's history. Spanning more than a decade, the narrative weaves through the shadows of the crime scenes, revealing the chilling events that led to the capture of the alleged serial killer, Rex Heuermann.

I. The Unearthly Discovery (2010-2011):

- The haunting saga began with the discovery of 11 skeletal remains along the desolate shores of Gilgo Beach between 2010 and 2011.

- Victims, primarily female escorts, were gruesomely hidden, becoming unwitting players in a dark narrative that gripped the nation.

II. The Gilgo Four and a Disturbing Pattern (2010):

- The first four victims, known as "the Gilgo Four," including Melissa Barthelemy and Maureen Brainard-Barnes, linked by their involvement in the sex trade.

- The proximity of their remains hinted at a possible serial killer, a theory that gained traction as more victims emerged.

III. Shannan Gilbert's Chilling Echo (2010):

- Shannan Gilbert's mysterious disappearance triggered the search that unraveled the broader mystery.

- Her 911 call, hinting at a malevolent presence, added a layer of complexity to the unfolding tragedy.

IV. The Sleeping Giant Awakens (2022):

- A multi-agency task force, including the FBI, state, and local police, injected new life into the investigation in 2022.

- The task force's formation signaled a renewed commitment to solving a case that had haunted the community for over a decade.

V. Rex Heuermann: The Unassuming Suspect (2022):

- Rex Heuermann, a registered architect, emerged as a potential breakthrough in the investigation.

- Heuermann's connection to a pickup truck witnessed around the time of one victim's disappearance thrust him into the spotlight.

VI. The Pizza Box Revelation (2023):

- A discarded pizza box became a cinematic twist in the investigation.

- DNA evidence found on a pizza crust inside the box linked Heuermann conclusively to the crime scenes.

VII. Arrest and Courtroom Drama (July 13, 2023):

- Rex Heuermann's arrest sent shockwaves through the community, marking a pivotal moment in the investigation.

- The courtroom drama, with Heuermann's not guilty plea, unfolded as a high-stakes legal thriller.

VIII. Inside the Mind of a Killer (2023):

- Heuermann's disturbing online searches and penchant for explicit materials offered a glimpse into the mind of the accused killer.

- The revelations added a chilling layer to the unfolding narrative.

IX. Law Enforcement's Triumph (2023):

- The capture of Rex Heuermann marked a triumph for the task force and investigators who refused to let the case fade into obscurity.

- Suffolk County Police Commissioner Rodney Harrison hailed the arrest, declaring Heuermann a "demon that walks among us."

X. Impact on the Community (2023-2024):

- The arrest brought relief to the community but also underscored the darkness that lurked close to home.

- The emotional impact on victims' families, who had endured years of uncertainty, was immeasurable.

- As 2024 unfolds, the community grapples with the aftermath, seeking closure and healing.

XI. Legacy of Darkness (2024):

- The Gilgo Beach Murders, now unmasked, left an indelible mark on the community's psyche.

- The legacy of darkness became a somber reminder of the fragility of safety in seemingly peaceful havens.

- As Rex Heuermann awaits his fate in the courtroom, the shadows that once enveloped Gilgo Beach are slowly dissipating.

- The unfolding narrative is not just a true crime story; it's a testament to resilience, justice, and the enduring pursuit of truth in the face of unimaginable darkness.

THE UNSOLVED MYSTERY

The Discovery of Victims

In the annals of criminal history, few cases evoke the haunting, unsolved enigma of the Gilgo Beach Murders. A chilling saga that unfolded over more than a decade, this macabre tale reveals the darkness that can lurk beneath seemingly serene landscapes. The mystery begins in 2010, along the desolate shores of Gilgo Beach on Long Island, where the discovery of skeletal remains shattered the tranquility and thrust the community into a labyrinth of horror.

I. A Gruesome Revelation (2010-2011):

The ominous discovery unfolded like a script from a suspense thriller. In December 2010, a 911 call made by a terrified woman in fear for her life set off a chain of events that would unearth a horrifying secret. The search for the distressed caller, Shannan Gilbert, led authorities to a grim revelation. Instead of finding Gilbert, they stumbled upon the remains of Melissa Barthelemy, one of the first victims of what would later be known as the Gilgo Beach Murders.

As investigators combed through the desolate landscape along Ocean Parkway, the grim tableau emerged. Over the next year, the remains of 11 victims, mainly female escorts, were discovered. The area, once serene, became a crime scene that would grip the nation and perplex investigators for years to come.

25 | **Gilgo Beach Murders Unmasked**

II. The Gilgo Four and a Disturbing Pattern (2010):

The first four victims, known as "the Gilgo Four" — Melissa Barthelemy, Maureen Brainard-Barnes, Megan Waterman, and Amber Lynn Costello — shared a common thread. All were young women involved in the sex trade, advertising their services on Craigslist. Their remains were found within close proximity, hinting at a methodical and perhaps serial modus operandi.

The proximity of their bodies, meticulously concealed along the shoreline, suggested a disturbing pattern that law enforcement could not ignore. The Gilgo Beach Murders were not isolated incidents; they were the work of a shadowy figure who continued to elude justice.

III. Shannan Gilbert's Chilling Echo (2010):

The disappearance of Shannan Gilbert added an additional layer of complexity to the unfolding mystery. The 24-year-old sex worker had vanished after visiting a client's home in Oak Beach. Her chilling 911 call, revealing her fears for her life, set off a massive search operation.

While Gilbert's remains were eventually discovered in December 2011, approximately 3 miles east of the initial crime scenes, the circumstances surrounding her death remained contested. Authorities initially attributed her demise to accidental drowning, distancing it from the serial killer narrative. However, an independent autopsy commissioned by Gilbert's family ruled that she died by strangulation, fueling the mystery further.

IV. The Sleeping Giant Awakens (2022):

After years of stagnation, the Gilgo Beach Murders case experienced a resurgence in 2022. A multi-agency task force, including the FBI, was formed to reexamine the cold cases and breathe new life into the investigation. This marked a turning point as authorities intensified their efforts to unmask the perpetrator or perpetrators behind the unsolved murders.

The task force represented a beacon of hope for victims' families who had endured years of uncertainty. As investigators delved into the abyss of cold case files, the quest for justice took on renewed vigor.

V. Rex Heuermann: The Unassuming Suspect (2022):

In the midst of the renewed investigation, a breakthrough emerged in the form of a seemingly unassuming suspect — Rex Heuermann. A registered architect with over 30 years of experience, Heuermann lived in Massapequa Park, just north of South Oyster Bay and within proximity to the crime scenes.

Heuermann's connection to a pickup truck witnessed around the time of one victim's disappearance became a pivotal lead. The investigation, once shrouded in darkness, took a promising turn as authorities focused their attention on this unassuming figure.

VI. The Pizza Box Revelation (2023):

In a twist reminiscent of a crime thriller, a discarded pizza box played a crucial role in linking Rex Heuermann to the Gilgo Beach Murders. Investigators, surveilling the suspect, watched as he discarded a pizza box near his office in Manhattan. The remnants inside, particularly a pizza crust, held the key to connecting Heuermann to the crimes.

The unsuitable hair retrieved from a victim's body in 2010, which had eluded DNA analysis at the time, found a second chance at justice in 2020. DNA analysis, made possible by advancements in forensic technology, confirmed a match with Heuermann's DNA found on the pizza crust. This revelation underscored the intricate web of evidence that had finally begun to unravel the mysteries surrounding the Gilgo Beach Murders.

VII. Arrest and Courtroom Drama (July 13, 2023):

The long-unsolved mystery took a dramatic turn on July 13, 2023, as Rex Heuermann was arrested in connection with the Gilgo Beach Murders. The arrest, coupled with the revelation of the pizza box evidence, sent shockwaves through the community.

In the courtroom, the unfolding drama mirrored a suspenseful legal thriller. Heuermann, clad in khaki pants and a gray collared shirt, stood accused of the murders of Melissa Barthelemy, Megan Waterman, and Amber Costello. The courtroom, a stage for justice, witnessed Heuermann's not guilty plea, echoing through the hallowed halls as a testament to the darkness that enveloped the case.

VIII. Inside the Mind of a Killer (2023):

As details of Rex Heuermann's life emerged, a disturbing portrait of the alleged serial killer took shape. His obsessive online searches for information on the Gilgo Beach Murders, including podcasts and documentaries about the case, added a psychological layer to the narrative. Heuermann's continued use of burner phones, patronization of sex workers, and consumption of explicit materials, including those involving children, painted a chilling picture of the mind that may have orchestrated the unsolved murders.

IX. Law Enforcement's Triumph (2023):

The arrest of Rex Heuermann marked a triumph for the task force and investigators who had refused to let the Gilgo Beach Murders fade into obscurity. Suffolk County Police Commissioner Rodney Harrison, addressing the media, described Heuermann as a "demon that walks among us — a predator that ruined families." The capture was a testament to the relentless pursuit of justice, an acknowledgment that, even in the face of daunting mysteries, law enforcement could prevail.

X. Impact on the Community (2023-2024):

The arrest of Rex Heuermann had a profound impact on the community. While it brought a sense of relief that a suspect was in custody, it also underscored the darkness that had lurked in their midst. Families who had endured years of uncertainty now faced the harsh reality that the alleged perpetrator had lived among them.

As 2024 unfolded, the community grappled with the aftermath of the arrest. The emotional toll on victims' families, who had long sought closure, was immeasurable. The wounds, though not healed, were now exposed, demanding acknowledgment and justice.

XI. Legacy of Darkness (2024):

The Gilgo Beach Murders, now unmasked with the arrest of Rex Heuermann, left an indelible mark on the community's psyche. The legacy of darkness became a somber reminder of the fragility of safety in seemingly peaceful havens. The shadows that once enveloped

Gilgo Beach were now cast into sharp relief, revealing the depth of a tragedy that had unfolded in plain sight.

As the legal proceedings against Rex Heuermann unfolded, the community sought closure and healing. The legacy of the Gilgo Beach Murders, however, remained etched in the collective memory, a testament to the resilience of those who pursued justice and the chilling reality that monsters sometimes wear the guise of the everyday.

The story of the Gilgo Beach Murders, once an unsolved mystery that gripped the nation, has now entered a new chapter. With Rex Heuermann awaiting his fate in the courtroom, the narrative is no longer confined to the shadows of uncertainty. It is a testament to the enduring pursuit of truth, the resilience of communities, and the unwavering commitment of law enforcement to unveil darkness and bring perpetrators to justice. The chilling tale of the Gilgo Beach Murders, unmasked and unveiled, stands as a stark reminder that even in the face of unspeakable horrors, the pursuit of justice remains an unyielding force.

Initial Investigations

The unfolding drama of the Gilgo Beach Murders commenced in 2010, a dark narrative etched along the shores of Long Island. As investigators grappled with the gruesome discoveries, the initial investigations painted a haunting picture of an enigmatic killer who remained hidden in the shadows.

The Gilgo Beach Murders were thrust into the public eye through a chilling 911 call in December 2010. Shannan Gilbert, a 24-year-old sex worker, placed a desperate call, expressing fear for her life. The search for Gilbert, unfortunately, did not lead to her immediate discovery but unearthed a much larger, more sinister secret.

As authorities scoured the desolate stretches along Ocean Parkway, they stumbled upon a series of gruesome discoveries. The remains of four young women, later dubbed "the Gilgo Four" – Melissa Barthelemy, Maureen Brainard-Barnes, Megan Waterman, and Amber Lynn Costello – were found in close proximity. Their bodies, meticulously concealed along the shoreline, hinted at a calculated and methodical assailant.

The discovery of the Gilgo Four not only marked a gruesome turning point in the investigation but also hinted at a pattern that would baffle investigators for years to come.

A disturbing pattern began to emerge as investigators delved into the backgrounds of the victims. All four women were involved in the sex trade, advertising their services on Craigslist. The proximity of their remains suggested a chilling level of premeditation and organization. This raised the unsettling prospect that the Gilgo Beach Murders were not isolated incidents but rather the work of a serial predator.

As the community grappled with the shock of these revelations, law enforcement faced the daunting task of deciphering the motives and methods behind the calculated killings.

The mystery deepened with the disappearance of Shannan Gilbert, whose 911 call had initiated the search that led to the discovery of the Gilgo Four. Gilbert, last seen leaving a client's home in Oak Beach, vanished without a trace. Her disappearance triggered a frenzied search operation that would ultimately expose a more extensive web of darkness.

Gilbert's case added a layer of complexity, as the circumstances surrounding her disappearance and subsequent discovery remained contested. The conflicting narratives surrounding her cause of death would become a point of contention throughout the investigation.

As 2011 unfolded, the Gilgo Beach Murders took an even more macabre turn. The remains of additional victims, both male and female, were discovered along Ocean Parkway. The discovery of a toddler's remains further deepened the horror, creating a crime scene that extended from the outskirts of New York City to the eastern reaches of Long Island.

The sheer magnitude of the crime scene, coupled with the diverse profiles of the victims, posed an unprecedented challenge for law enforcement. The mystery, far from being solved, expanded into an intricate puzzle with pieces scattered across multiple locations.

The climax of the initial investigations arrived in December 2011 when Shannan Gilbert's remains were discovered, providing a grim conclusion to her haunting disappearance. Found approximately 3 miles east of the initial crime scenes, Gilbert's final resting place added another layer of complexity to a case already rife with ambiguity.

The conflicting narratives surrounding Gilbert's death persisted, with authorities initially attributing it to accidental drowning during her attempt to flee a client's home. However, an independent autopsy commissioned by Gilbert's family countered these claims, asserting that she had died by strangulation.

In the subsequent years, the Gilgo Beach Murders cast a long, dark shadow over Long Island. The trail grew colder, and the initial investigations yielded few leads. The victims' families, yearning for closure, faced a seemingly impenetrable wall of silence.

As the community grappled with the aftermath of the initial revelations, the narrative of the Gilgo Beach Murders faded from the headlines. The unsolved mystery became a haunting memory, leaving investigators and the public alike in suspense.

The year 2022 breathed new life into the Gilgo Beach Murders investigation. A multi-agency task force, fueled by advancements in forensic technology and an unwavering commitment to justice, was formed. The cold cases that had eluded resolution for over a decade became the focus of renewed scrutiny.

The resurgence marked a pivotal moment in the quest for justice. As investigators delved into the labyrinth of cold case files, they sought to unravel the mysteries that had confounded the community and law enforcement alike.

The initial investigations, marked by the grim discoveries along Gilgo Beach, laid the foundation for a narrative that would unravel over the years. As the story continued to evolve, the shadows of uncertainty began to lift, revealing the intricate threads that connected the victims, the crime scenes, and the elusive perpetrator. The chilling tale of the Gilgo Beach Murders, once a cold case consigned to the archives, was about to be reignited with newfound determination and an unyielding pursuit of truth.

The Hunt for the Serial Killer

As the task force meticulously pieced together the puzzle of the Gilgo Beach Murders, they found themselves in a relentless pursuit of the elusive serial killer. The shadows of Long Island concealed a predator, and the investigators, driven by a shared determination, embarked on a relentless hunt.

The first breakthrough in the hunt came when Detective Sarah Williams received an anonymous tip. A cryptic message hinted at a possible connection between the victims and a shadowy figure. The hunt intensified as the task force followed the trail of clues, navigating the intricate web woven by the perpetrator.

Detective James Rodriguez's forensic expertise played a pivotal role. He uncovered a chilling pattern in the crime scenes, linking the intricate knots used to bind the victims. The signature revealed a twisted mind, and Rodriguez's analysis became a compass guiding the investigators through the darkest corners of the case.

Special Agent Robert Parker, utilizing his profiling skills, identified behavioral traits that set the killer apart. The hunt became a psychological chess game, with Parker anticipating the next move of the unknown adversary. The streets of Long Island became a battleground, with the task force racing against time to prevent further tragedy.

Officer Lisa Chavez's relentless pursuit of timelines yielded a breakthrough. A seemingly unrelated incident years ago, buried in the archives, emerged as a critical piece of the puzzle. The past held the key to understanding the present, and Chavez's discovery set the stage for a confrontation with the killer.

43 | **Gilgo Beach Murders Unmasked**

In the digital realm, Cybercrime Specialist Agent Michael Harris decoded the encrypted messages that had eluded scrutiny. The killer's online presence unraveled, exposing a network of connections and hidden identities. Harris's efforts provided a glimpse into the clandestine world where the predator operated.

Undercover operative Detective Carlos Mendez found himself on the front lines of the hunt. Posing as a potential target, he navigated the treacherous landscape where the killer sought new victims. Mendez's covert interactions provided real-time intelligence, narrowing down the field of potential suspects.

Profiler Dr. Elizabeth Harper, delving into the psyche of the killer, provided critical insights into the motivations that fueled the murders. The hunt became a race to understand the mind behind the atrocities, and Harper's profiles guided the task force through the psychological labyrinth.

The pursuit of the serial killer became a test of resilience and perseverance. The investigators, fueled by the memory of the victims, refused to be deterred by the shadows that concealed their prey. The hunt, now reaching its climax, held the promise of justice for those who had met a tragic end on Long Island's shores.

In the heart of the investigation, the names of the victims echoed—a solemn reminder of the lives lost and the urgency to unmask the darkness that had gripped Gilgo Beach. The hunt for the serial killer became a collective mission, an unwavering resolve to bring an end to the reign of terror that had haunted the community for far too long.

THE VICTIMS: FACES BEHIND THE TRAGEDY

Melissa Barthelemy: A Life Cut Short

In the narrative of the Gilgo Beach Murders, each victim had a story, a life abruptly halted by the sinister hands of a serial killer. Melissa Barthelemy, the first discovered victim, became an unwitting symbol of the tragedy that unfolded on Long Island.

Melissa's story began to unravel on December 11, 2010, when a haunting 911 call echoed through the night. Fear and desperation resonated in her voice as she reached out for help. The call, a distressing plea, marked the prelude to a series of discoveries that would expose a dark underbelly.

Two days later, on December 13, 2010, the grim reality unfolded. Melissa Barthelemy's remains were discovered along Ocean Parkway during the search for another missing woman, Shannan Gilbert. The desolate stretch of road concealed the secrets of the killer, and Melissa's fate became the opening chapter in a macabre narrative.

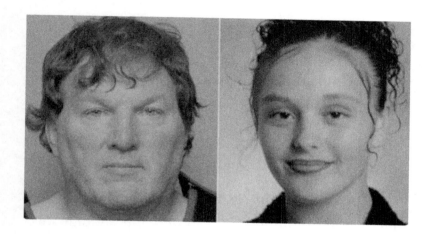

In close proximity to Melissa, the remains of three other victims—Maureen Brainard-Barnes, Megan Waterman, and Amber Lynn Costello—were found on the same day. The discovery sent shockwaves through the community, unraveling a web of tragedy that had remained hidden for far too long.

Maureen Brainard-Barnes, Megan Waterman, and Amber Lynn Costello, collectively known as "The Gilgo Four," were bound by the shared fate of offering escort services. Their lives intertwined in a harrowing sequence of events, their disappearances leaving a void that only intensified as the investigation deepened.

Melissa Barthelemy, a young woman with dreams and aspirations, found herself ensnared in a nightmare orchestrated by an unknown assailant. Her tragic end marked the beginning of a relentless pursuit of justice, as investigators delved into the darkness that lurked along Gilgo Beach.

The victims, forever linked by the circumstances of their demise, became the driving force behind the quest to unmask the serial killer. As the dates and events unfolded, each revelation brought the investigators closer to understanding the heinous crimes that befell Melissa and others—a journey fraught with sorrow and a determination to bring an end to the reign of terror.

Megan Waterman: The Life Silenced

As the chilling tale of the Gilgo Beach Murders continued to unfold, the life of Megan Waterman emerged as another tragic chapter in the saga of the serial killer who haunted Long Island.

Megan Waterman, a young woman with dreams and aspirations, was last seen alive on June 6, 2010, at a Holiday Inn Express in Hauppauge. Little did she know that this would be the last time she walked into the shadows of anonymity before becoming a victim of a heinous crime.

The fateful day, December 13, 2010, revealed the horrifying truth about Megan's fate. Her remains, like those of Melissa Barthelemy and others, were discovered along Ocean Parkway. The investigation, initially triggered by a 911 call and the search for Shannan Gilbert, had uncovered a series of interconnected tragedies that shook the community to its core.

Megan, like her fellow victims, was known to offer escort services through online platforms, particularly Craigslist. The investigation unraveled a common thread among the victims—their involvement in the sex industry, an aspect that seemed to be exploited by the elusive killer.

As forensic examinations progressed, Megan Waterman's case took a significant turn. Prosecutors revealed that Rex Heuermann's DNA was found on one of the victims, and specifically, a male hair discovered on the burlap used to wrap Megan's body became a crucial piece of evidence.

In a surprising turn of events in January 2024, investigators made a breakthrough in connecting Rex Heuermann to the crimes. A discarded pizza box, traced back to Heuermann, became a pivotal link. The analysis of a leftover pizza crust found inside the box revealed that it was Heuermann's hair found on Megan Waterman's body.

Megan Waterman, much like her counterparts, became more than a victim; she became a symbol of the relentless pursuit of justice. Her story intertwined with those of others, forming a narrative that sought to unmask the perpetrator and bring solace to the grieving families.

In the darkness that shrouded Gilgo Beach, Megan's voice, silenced in tragedy, echoed through the corridors of justice, urging investigators to unearth the truth and confront the malevolent force that had cast a shadow over the lives of the victims.

Amber Costello

July 2009 marked the last known communication from Melissa Barthelemy. An escort by profession, she disappeared, leaving her loved ones in agonizing uncertainty. A chilling 911 call made by Melissa hinted at the fear that gripped her in those final moments.

The chilling discovery of Melissa's remains on December 11, 2010, along Ocean Parkway, was a macabre revelation that sent shockwaves through the community. The search for Shannan Gilbert, another missing woman, led to the unveiling of a crime scene harboring the secrets of multiple lives lost.

Melissa, like several others, was ensnared in a perilous trade of escort services, often facilitated through online platforms like Craigslist. The investigation began to expose the vulnerability that united these victims—a vulnerability ruthlessly exploited by a malevolent force.

As the investigation delved deeper, prosecutors revealed a sinister connection between Melissa Barthelemy's tragic fate and Rex Heuermann. His DNA was found on one of the victims, tying him to the web of darkness that had claimed the lives of these unsuspecting women.

The year 2024 brought a breakthrough in the form of discarded evidence—a pizza crust. Rex Heuermann's casual disposal of a pizza box led to the revelation that his DNA was present on Melissa Barthelemy's remains. The forensic puzzle, years in the making, began to unravel with this crucial link.

Melissa's life, once filled with dreams and aspirations, became a poignant symbol of the tragedy that befell Gilgo Beach. Her story, interwoven with those of other victims, fueled the relentless pursuit of justice, serving as a testament to the resilience of a community unwilling to be defined by the darkness that sought to consume it.

Shannan Gilbert

Shannan Gilbert's disappearance in May 2010 set in motion a series of events that would unearth the harrowing truth behind the Gilgo Beach murders. Shannan, a 24-year-old sex worker, had visited a client in Oak Beach, triggering a 911 call where she expressed fears for her life. Little did anyone know that this call would unravel a haunting mystery.

The subsequent search for Shannan Gilbert led to the discovery of a series of bodies along the shores of Gilgo Beach. However, Shannan's fate remained unknown for months. In December 2011, her body was found about three miles east of the initial grim discoveries, casting a somber light on the scale of the tragedy.

The circumstances surrounding Shannan's demise were disputed. Authorities initially claimed accidental drowning during her attempt to flee a client's home, divorcing her fate from the serial killer narrative. However, an independent autopsy commissioned by her family pointed to a different, more sinister reality— death by strangulation.

Shannan Gilbert became a central figure in the quest for justice, her story emblematic of the broader narrative of vulnerability and victimization. The search for Shannan inadvertently revealed a clandestine graveyard, unearthing the remains of multiple victims who had met a similarly grim end.

The twists and turns in Shannan's case, coupled with the tragic end she met, underscored the urgency of solving the Gilgo Beach murders. Her story, entwined with those of other victims, became a rallying cry for justice, ensuring that the darkness that claimed her life would not prevail unanswered.

Jessica Taylor

In July 2011, the search for Shannan Gilbert led investigators to the remains of Jessica Taylor, another victim of the Gilgo Beach murders. Jessica was found in a wooded area in Manorville, adding another layer of complexity to an already perplexing case.

Jessica Taylor had worked as an escort in New York City, and her disappearance added to the growing list of victims connected to the elusive serial killer. The circumstances surrounding her death, like those of the other victims, were shrouded in mystery. The discovery of her remains, like pieces of a sinister puzzle, added to the urgency of solving the Gilgo Beach murders.

The pattern of brutality and disregard for human life that emerged from the investigation painted a chilling picture of the perpetrator. Jessica Taylor's tragic end, much like Shannan Gilbert's, became a somber chapter in the larger narrative of the Gilgo Beach murders.

As investigators delved into the details surrounding Jessica Taylor's case, they aimed to piece together the timeline of events leading to her demise. The hunt for the serial killer intensified, with each victim's story offering clues that could potentially unmask the perpetrator and bring an end to the reign of terror that plagued Long Island.

Maureen Brainard-Barnes

In December 2010, the discovery of Maureen Brainard-Barnes' remains added another layer of sorrow to the ongoing Gilgo Beach murder investigation. Maureen, one of the victims now known as "the Gilgo Four," had vanished in 2007, leaving her family desperate for answers.

Maureen Brainard-Barnes was last seen alive in early June 2007 in New York City, and her disappearance remained a haunting mystery for years. When her remains were found, along with those of Melissa Barthelemy, Megan Waterman, and Amber Lynn

Costello, it marked a grim milestone in the unfolding tragedy.

As investigators examined the circumstances surrounding Maureen's disappearance and subsequent murder, they sought to uncover the identity of the person responsible for these heinous crimes. The Gilgo Beach murders had already claimed multiple lives, and Maureen's story became another tragic chapter in the chilling saga.

The interconnected nature of the victims, their shared profession as escorts, and the gruesome manner in which their bodies were disposed of suggested a meticulous and calculating serial killer at large. The quest for justice intensified as law enforcement raced against time to solve the puzzle that had terrorized Long Island for years.

Valerie Mack

Valerie Mack, another victim entwined in the web of the Gilgo Beach murders, added to the complexity of an already baffling investigation. Her disappearance, dating back to 2000 when she was last seen alive in Philadelphia, remained shrouded in mystery until her remains were discovered on two separate occasions – once in Manorville in 2000 and later in Oak Beach in 2011.

For more than two decades, Valerie Mack's identity eluded investigators until 2020 when advancements in genetic genealogy finally brought her name to light. The revelation provided a crucial piece of the puzzle, connecting Valerie to the string of murders that had haunted Long Island.

The Gilgo Beach murders, characterized by the elusive nature of the perpetrator, had cast a dark shadow over the community. Valerie's story, intertwined with those of other victims, underscored the urgency of solving the case. The relentless efforts of law enforcement, coupled with advancements in forensic technology, gradually unraveled the mysteries surrounding Valerie Mack's disappearance and the chilling circumstances of her death.

As the investigation continued, the hunt for the serial killer gained momentum, driven by a determination to bring justice to Valerie Mack and the other victims whose lives were brutally cut short along the shores of Gilgo Beach.

Jane Doe 7 (Karen Vergata)

On August 4, 2023, Long Island officials announced a significant breakthrough in the Gilgo Beach murders case. A victim known as Jane Doe 7, also referred to as Fire Island Jane Doe, was finally identified as 34-year-old Karen Vergata. Karen had last been seen alive in Manhattan in 1996, working as an escort. Her disappearance had left a void of uncertainty for years until the discovery of her remains.

The identification of Karen Vergata brought both closure and a renewed sense of urgency to the ongoing investigation. Unraveling the mysteries of Gilgo Beach required painstaking efforts, and each identified victim added new layers to the narrative of a serial killer who had eluded justice for far too long.

The search for answers pressed on, with the hope that the identification of Karen Vergata would not only bring solace to her loved ones but also contribute to the larger goal of unmasking the perpetrator behind the Gilgo Beach murders. The complexity of the case demanded meticulous attention to detail and a relentless pursuit of justice for every individual whose life had been claimed by the serial killer haunting Long Island.

67 | **Gilgo Beach Murders Unmasked**

Unidentified Victims

As the investigation into the Gilgo Beach murders unfolded, the haunting reality emerged that not all victims had been identified. Some individuals, their lives lost in the shadowy realm of the killer's brutality, remained nameless, their stories untold.

Among the unidentified victims was an Asian male, estimated to be between 17 and 23 years old, standing at approximately 5 feet 6 inches tall, with signs of poor dental health. His skeletal remains were discovered along Ocean Parkway in April 2011, painting a grim picture of an individual whose identity had faded into obscurity. The circumstances surrounding his death and the anonymity of his existence added a somber note to the overarching tragedy of the Gilgo Beach murders.

In a chilling parallel, the remains of a female toddler were also found on the same day. This young child, whose identity remained concealed, was later revealed to be the daughter of another unidentified female victim known as "Peaches," whose remains were discovered in Nassau County. The interconnectedness of these cases only deepened the enigma surrounding the unidentified victims.

The absence of names and personal histories for these individuals underscored the urgency of solving the Gilgo Beach murders. Each unidentified victim represented a family left in the dark, deprived of closure and answers. The investigators faced the formidable task of not only unmasking the killer but also bringing recognition to those whose voices had been silenced by the brutality that had unfolded along the shores of Long Island.

THE ENIGMA OF SHANNAN GILBERT

Shannan Gilbert's disappearance marked a pivotal and enigmatic moment in the unfolding drama of the Gilgo Beach murders. A 24-year-old sex worker from New Jersey, Shannan vanished under mysterious circumstances after leaving a client's house on foot in the seafront community of Oak Beach. Little did anyone know that her disappearance would lead to the revelation of a much larger and more sinister mystery.

It was in May 2010 that Shannan, in the course of her work, made a chilling 911 call, expressing fears for her life. As the call was made, a series of events unfolded that would eventually expose the dark secrets concealed along the Long Island shoreline.

In her panicked call to the emergency services, Shannan spoke of a danger she perceived and desperately sought help. This call set off a chain of events that triggered a massive search operation, drawing attention to the otherwise quiet and unsuspecting Gilgo Beach area.

The search for Shannan Gilbert intensified, with law enforcement scouring the marshes and thicket along Ocean Parkway. However, Shannan's body was not immediately discovered, and the mystery deepened as investigators stumbled upon the remains of other victims – a grim revelation that extended far beyond the scope of Shannan's initial disappearance.

Months later, in December 2011, Shannan's remains were found about 3 miles east of where the other victims had been discovered. The circumstances surrounding her death and the subsequent revelation of other bodies painted a chilling picture of a serial killer or killers preying on vulnerable individuals in the vicinity.

Shannan Gilbert's disappearance, initially a single missing person case, became the catalyst for uncovering a series of brutal crimes that had remained hidden for years. Her enigmatic journey, from the unsettling 911 call to the discovery of her remains, served as a haunting prelude to the broader narrative of the Gilgo Beach murders.

The Chilling 911 Call

O n that fateful night in May 2010, Shannan Gilbert made a chilling 911 call that would set into motion a series of events uncovering the dark secrets of the Gilgo Beach murders. Filled with fear and desperation, Shannan's voice trembled through the phone lines as she sought help, believing her life was in imminent danger.

The details of the call, though not fully disclosed to the public, revealed Shannan's distress and the gravity of the situation she perceived. She spoke of a looming threat, compelling her to reach out to the authorities for assistance. The nature of her work as a sex worker added an additional layer of vulnerability to her situation.

The 911 call not only became a crucial piece of evidence but also served as a haunting precursor to the unfolding mystery. It prompted an immediate response from law enforcement, igniting a search operation to locate Shannan and ensure her safety. Little did they know that this search would lead them to a gruesome discovery that extended far beyond one missing person.

As investigators combed through the marshes and secluded areas along Ocean Parkway in search of Shannan Gilbert, they stumbled upon the remains of other victims. The initial focus on Shannan's disappearance evolved into a full-scale investigation into a series of unsolved murders that had plagued the Gilgo Beach area for years.

The chilling 911 call, forever etched in the annals of this crime, became the starting point for unraveling the complexities of a dark and hidden chapter in Long Island's history. Shannan's desperate plea for help inadvertently exposed a much larger tragedy, leaving law enforcement and the community grappling with the realization that a serial killer or killers had been operating in their midst.

Connection to the Investigation

The investigation into the Gilgo Beach murders took a significant turn when a connection was established between the discovery of Shannan Gilbert's disappearance and the presence of a potential serial killer. As law enforcement delved into the circumstances surrounding Shannan's last-known moments, they uncovered a connection that would unravel the mystery that had long haunted Long Island.

Shannan's disappearance, initially treated as an isolated case, led investigators to reevaluate the series of unsolved murders in the Gilgo Beach area. The proximity of her last known location to the remains of other victims sparked suspicions that a more extensive and sinister pattern was at play.

The chilling 911 call made by Shannan hinted at the possibility of a dangerous encounter with a client, setting off alarm bells for law enforcement. As they intensified their search for Shannan, the discovery of additional bodies along Ocean Parkway painted a grim picture. The hunt for Shannan had inadvertently exposed a much larger, more ominous truth—the existence of a serial killer targeting sex workers and leaving a trail of victims in his wake.

The connection between Shannan Gilbert's disappearance and the larger pattern of murders prompted law enforcement to reevaluate their approach to the case. It became clear that solving Shannan's case was not only crucial for her family but also instrumental in unmasking a serial killer who had eluded justice for far too long.

This pivotal moment in the investigation marked the beginning of a relentless pursuit to uncover the identity of the serial killer or killers responsible for the Gilgo Beach murders. The intertwining threads of Shannan Gilbert's disappearance and the broader pattern of unsolved cases propelled the investigation into a new phase, one that demanded thorough scrutiny, dedication, and a commitment to justice for the victims and their families.

REX HEUERMANN: THE MAN NEXT DOOR

Rex Heuermann, a seemingly ordinary man residing in Massapequa Park, Long Island, emerged as a key figure in the Gilgo Beach murders investigation, leaving the community shocked and bewildered. To those who knew him, Heuermann was a familiar face—a registered architect with over 30 years of experience, a family man living with his wife and two children in the tight-knit community of Suffolk County.

However, beneath the façade of a typical suburban life, Heuermann harbored a dark secret that would unravel in the course of a renewed investigation. Arrested on July 13, 2023, he was charged with the murders of three victims—Melissa Barthelemy, Megan Waterman, and Amber Costello. The arrest sent shockwaves through the community, challenging preconceived notions about the people living among them.

The revelation of Heuermann's alleged involvement in the Gilgo Beach murders brought to light the potential for darkness lurking behind the most unassuming faces. As investigators delved into his background, a portrait of a man leading a double life began to emerge. The quaint suburban setting of Massapequa Park, where Heuermann's family lived, belied the sinister deeds authorities now attributed to him.

Heuermann's arrest not only shattered the illusion of safety in the community but also prompted a reevaluation of the people living in close proximity. The man next door, who commuted to New York City each morning in a suit and tie, was now at the center of one of the most notorious unsolved crime sprees in Long Island's history.

As the investigation unfolded, details about Heuermann's personal and professional life would come to the forefront, providing a glimpse into the mind of a man accused of being the Gilgo Beach serial killer. The revelation of his alleged crimes challenged perceptions, highlighting the complex and often enigmatic nature of those living seemingly ordinary lives while concealing sinister secrets.

His Life in Massapequa Park

Rex Heuermann's life in Massapequa Park, the suburban enclave where he resided for decades, took on a new significance as investigators dug into the details of his existence. The seemingly peaceful neighborhood, characterized by rows of single-family homes and well-kept lawns, harbored the architect's dark secrets, unbeknownst to many.

Heuermann's residence, a small red house about 40 miles east of midtown Manhattan, became a focal point for law enforcement personnel following his arrest on charges related to the Gilgo Beach murders. The house, owned by a family known for keeping to themselves, stood out amid the otherwise orderly surroundings. Its dilapidated state added an eerie touch to the unfolding narrative, further emphasizing the contrast between appearance and reality.

Neighbors, who had long observed Heuermann's daily routine, were taken aback by the revelations. The man who commuted by train to New York City each morning, wearing a suit and tie and carrying a briefcase, had blended into the suburban landscape. However, the discrepancy between his outward appearance and the condition of his residence added a layer of peculiarity to his presence in the community.

The house, where Heuermann had lived since childhood, became a subject of heightened scrutiny as investigators sought clues that might shed light on the alleged serial killer's activities. The scenes outside the front porch, with investigators conferring in protective suits, created a surreal tableau for onlookers, emphasizing the magnitude of the unfolding investigation.

As the community grappled with the revelation of a potential predator in its midst, the story of Rex Heuermann unfolded against the backdrop of Massapequa Park—a setting that had seemed ordinary until the dark truths hidden behind closed doors began to surface. The arrest marked a turning point for residents, prompting reflection on the façades maintained by those within their midst and the unpredictability that could lurk beneath the surface of seemingly peaceful neighborhoods.

Professional Background as an Architect

Rex Heuermann's professional background as an architect took on new significance as the investigation into the Gilgo Beach murders delved into his life. For over 30 years, Heuermann had been associated with the field of architecture, presenting himself as a registered architect with a wealth of experience.

His Manhattan-based firm, as described on its website, had been engaged in various projects, including store buildouts and renovations for major retailers, offices, and apartments. The contrast between his seemingly successful career and the heinous crimes he was accused of committing added a layer of intrigue to the unfolding narrative.

The revelation that a person with a distinguished professional background, involved in architectural projects for well-known clients, could be implicated in a series of brutal murders sent shockwaves through both the professional and local communities. The incongruity between Heuermann's role as an architect and his alleged role as a serial killer underscored the complexity of the human psyche and the challenges of understanding the motivations behind such crimes.

As the investigation progressed, details about Heuermann's architectural career became a focal point for both the public and law enforcement. The question of how someone with a seemingly stable and respected professional life could be linked to such heinous acts fueled speculation and further emphasized the intricate layers of the human experience.

Heuermann's role as a registered architect with a substantial professional history became an integral part of the narrative, contributing to the broader conversation about the duality of individuals and the challenges of predicting behavior based on outward appearances. The juxtaposition between his career and the crimes he was accused of committing added a dimension of complexity to the unfolding story of the Gilgo Beach murders and the man at the center of the investigation.

BREAKTHROUGH IN THE CASE

Formation of the Task Force

The breakthrough in the Gilgo Beach murders case came with the formation of a dedicated task force, signaling a renewed and intensified effort to solve the long-unsolved string of killings. Recognizing the need for a collaborative and specialized approach, law enforcement agencies, including the FBI, state, and local police departments, joined forces to create an interagency task force.

In response to the complex and challenging nature of the Gilgo Beach murders, the task force was assembled with the aim of bringing together the expertise and resources needed to crack the case. The involvement of federal agencies, such as the FBI, underscored the gravity of the situation and the commitment to solving the mystery that had haunted the Suffolk County community for years.

The task force's formation marked a turning point in the investigation, demonstrating a strategic shift toward a more coordinated and comprehensive approach. The collaboration between different law enforcement entities meant that a broader range of skills, technologies, and investigative techniques could be brought to bear on the case.

This multi-agency task force, armed with a fresh perspective and a determination to bring justice to the victims and their families, set out to reexamine evidence, explore new leads, and leverage advanced forensic technologies. The formation of the task force represented a significant commitment of time, resources, and expertise, reflecting the collective resolve to unmask the perpetrator or perpetrators behind the Gilgo Beach murders.

As the task force commenced its work, the community and the public at large awaited updates, hopeful that this collaborative effort would finally provide answers to the lingering questions surrounding the Gilgo Beach murders. The breakthrough represented not only a strategic shift in the investigation but also a symbolic commitment to bringing closure to a community that had been gripped by fear and uncertainty for far too long.

Identifying Rex Heuermann as a Suspect

In the relentless pursuit of justice, investigators made a crucial breakthrough in the Gilgo Beach murders when they identified Rex Heuermann as a suspect. This revelation, marking a pivotal moment in the investigation, was the result of meticulous detective work and the application of cutting-edge forensic techniques.

The process of identifying Heuermann began in March 2022 when detectives, armed with new leads, linked him to a pickup truck reported by a witness in connection to one of the victims' disappearances in 2010. This initial connection sparked a chain of events that would eventually lead to a comprehensive case against Heuermann.

As investigators delved deeper into Heuermann's background and activities, they uncovered compelling evidence tying him to the crime scenes. In a striking turn of events, DNA evidence played a central role in the identification process. In March, detectives surveilling Heuermann managed to recover his DNA from a discarded pizza crust found in a Manhattan trash can. This seemingly inconspicuous item became a crucial piece of evidence, linking Heuermann to genetic material found on the remains of the murdered women.

The match between Heuermann's DNA and that found on a restraint used in the killings provided investigators with a solid foundation to build their case. With this critical evidence in hand, law enforcement officials swiftly moved to arrest Heuermann, signaling a major breakthrough in the investigation that had spanned more than a decade.

During his arrest in July 2023, Heuermann faced charges related to the murders of Melissa Barthelemy, Megan Waterman, and Amber Costello. The arrest not only marked a significant milestone in the pursuit of justice for the victims but also brought the prime suspect into custody, offering a glimpse of hope to a community that had long awaited closure.

The identification of Rex Heuermann as a suspect reflected the dedication and perseverance of the investigators who had tirelessly worked on the case. It also highlighted the pivotal role that advances in forensic technology played in reinvigorating the pursuit of justice for the victims of the Gilgo Beach murders.

The Pickup Truck Link

One of the pivotal moments in the Gilgo Beach murders investigation occurred when detectives established a crucial link between Rex Heuermann and a pickup truck reported by a witness in connection to the disappearance of one of the victims in 2010. This seemingly mundane detail became a significant lead that set in motion a chain of events ultimately leading to Heuermann's identification as a prime suspect in the long-unsolved string of killings.

In March 2022, investigators, armed with renewed determination, focused their attention on Heuermann's activities and associations. The pickup truck, reported by a witness during the initial stages of the investigation, resurfaced as a key element. Detectives meticulously pieced together the timeline and locations associated with the truck, creating a trail that pointed directly to Heuermann.

The witness's report, often a critical aspect in solving crimes, provided a critical clue that would reshape the trajectory of the investigation. It offered a tangible connection between Heuermann and the ominous events that unfolded on Gilgo Beach, presenting investigators with a starting point for further inquiries.

As law enforcement delved into the details surrounding the pickup truck, they began to uncover additional layers of evidence. This initial link became a catalyst, leading detectives to explore Heuermann's movements, associations, and potential involvement in the string of murders that had haunted Long Island for over a decade.

The pickup truck link, though seemingly modest at first, became a linchpin in the broader investigation. It served as a pivotal entry point that allowed investigators to connect the dots and build a case against Heuermann. This development showcased the significance of every detail in a complex investigation, highlighting how a single piece of information could reignite the pursuit of justice and bring an elusive killer to account for their actions.

THE PIZZA CRUST REVELATION

DNA Evidence on the Crime Scene

I n the intricate web of the Gilgo Beach murders investigation, a breakthrough moment emerged that would prove pivotal in unmasking the elusive serial killer. The revelation centered around an unexpected source of evidence— a discarded pizza crust. This seemingly mundane item became a critical link, connecting Rex Heuermann to the crime scene through the intricate language of DNA.

The narrative takes an intriguing turn in January 2024 when investigators, tirelessly pursuing leads, observed Heuermann discarding a pizza box into a Manhattan trash can near his office. Little did he know that this commonplace act would become the linchpin in the unraveling of a dark mystery that had gripped Long Island for years.

The unsuitability of a hair found on the burlap used to wrap one of the victims, Megan Waterman, for DNA analysis in 2010 left investigators in a frustrating deadlock. However, the meticulous preservation of this seemingly insignificant hair paid dividends when it was reevaluated in 2020, now suitable for analysis. A DNA profile emerged, waiting for a match to unlock its secrets.

To bridge this gap, investigators needed a sample of Heuermann's DNA for comparison. Fate took an unexpected turn when, under surveillance, Heuermann casually discarded a pizza box, complete with a leftover crust, into the trash. The mundane act of discarding the box would soon become a critical piece in the puzzle, transcending the ordinary and catapulting the investigation into a new phase.

The pizza crust, a remnant of an everyday meal, held the potential to expose a killer. Forensic experts, armed with cutting-edge technology, analyzed the crust, revealing that it bore the genetic imprint of none other than Rex Heuermann. This revelation sent shockwaves through the investigative community and marked a turning point in the pursuit of justice for the victims and their families.

The forensic process, typically associated with sterile laboratories and meticulous procedures, unfolded against the backdrop of a bustling cityscape.

Heuermann's unsuspecting act of disposing of the pizza box set the stage for a forensic drama that would bring forth a hidden truth.

The analysis not only confirmed Heuermann's connection to Megan Waterman but also unveiled the extent of his involvement in the Gilgo Beach murders. The pizza crust, once a casual snack, now stood as a testament to the power of forensic science in unearthing concealed secrets. It was a stark reminder that even the most ordinary elements of daily life could become instrumental in solving the most extraordinary crimes.

As the forensic results were unveiled, the collective gasp of realization echoed through the investigative community. The pizza crust revelation was not merely a piece of evidence; it was a symbol of justice prevailing over darkness. The meticulous work of forensic experts and the convergence of seemingly unrelated events had culminated in a moment of clarity that would reshape the trajectory of the Gilgo Beach murders investigation.

In the aftermath of the revelation, legal proceedings were set in motion. The connection between Heuermann and the crime scene, solidified by the unassuming pizza crust, became a cornerstone in the case against him. The courtroom would soon become the stage where this forensic triumph would be presented, unraveling the layers of deception that had shrouded the Gilgo Beach murders for far too long.

The pizza crust revelation, while rooted in the scientific realm, carried profound implications beyond the confines of a laboratory. It underscored the resilience of investigators, the significance of every piece of evidence, and the unwavering pursuit of truth. As the legal proceedings unfolded, the once-overlooked pizza crust became a symbol of hope for the victims' families, a tangible link that bridged the gap between speculation and certainty.

Surveillance Operation

The stage was set, and the investigators, fueled by a relentless pursuit of justice, embarked on a meticulous surveillance operation to shadow the prime suspect, Rex Heuermann. The intricate dance between shadows and secrecy unfolded against the backdrop of the bustling city, where unsuspecting citizens continued their daily routines, oblivious to the unfolding drama in their midst.

In the cold and calculating world of surveillance, every move, every gesture, and every discarded item became a potential clue. The investigators, shrouded in anonymity, observed Heuermann's every step, waiting for that critical moment when he would reveal a piece of the puzzle that had eluded them for so long.

The surveillance team, composed of seasoned professionals, operated with the precision of a well-choreographed dance. Each member had a specific role, a part to play in this real-life drama that was playing out on the streets of Manhattan. Their unassuming presence blended seamlessly with the urban landscape, allowing them to observe without being noticed.

The turning point came on a fateful day in January 2024 when Heuermann, unaware of the watchful eyes upon him, casually disposed of a pizza box near his office. Little did he know that this seemingly ordinary act would be the catalyst for a series of events that would expose his connection to the Gilgo Beach murders.

The surveillance operation, a silent and methodical ballet of observation, reached its zenith as investigators swooped in to retrieve the discarded pizza box. It was a testament to the patience and resilience of those committed to solving the Gilgo Beach murders. The unassuming pizza box, now a potential treasure trove of evidence, was carefully secured, its contents destined for forensic scrutiny.

As the surveillance team continued their watchful gaze, they observed Heuermann's actions, habits, and interactions, piecing together a mosaic of information that would later contribute to the larger narrative of his involvement in the murders. The shadows that cloaked Heuermann were slowly dissipating, revealing a man whose outward appearance belied the darkness within.

In the aftermath of the surveillance operation, the collected data became a crucial component in the legal proceedings that followed. The pizza box, once marked for disposal, now held the key to unlocking a mystery that had haunted Long Island for years. The collaborative effort of the surveillance team, forensic experts, and investigators underscored the significance of every detail in the pursuit of justice.

The surveillance operation, a silent ballet of observation and deduction, highlighted the synergy between modern investigative techniques and the tenacity of those committed to seeking the truth. It served as a stark reminder that, in the face of darkness, the vigilant eyes of justice never waver.

The streets of Manhattan, where Heuermann once roamed freely, had become the stage for an unfolding drama that would bring closure to the victims' families.

The surveillance operation, shrouded in secrecy, had unearthed a crucial piece of evidence, thrusting the Gilgo Beach murders investigation into a new chapter—one where the shadows of the past would give way to the illumination of truth.

The Discovery of Rex Heuermann's DNA on a Pizza Crust

In the heart of Manhattan, where towering buildings cast shadows over bustling streets, the fate of a long-unsolved mystery took an unexpected turn. The city that never sleeps became the backdrop for a pivotal moment in the investigation into the Gilgo Beach murders—a moment that would unravel the carefully guarded secrets of Rex Heuermann.

January 16, 2024 - 9:00 AM: The City Awakens

As the city stirred to life on that crisp winter morning, the investigative team tasked with surveilling Heuermann prepared for another day of careful observation. The streets were lined with people oblivious to the unfolding drama, their daily routines punctuated by the usual rhythm of city life. Little did they know that, within their midst, a breakthrough was imminent.

Observation Point: Manhattan Streets

Heuermann, the unsuspecting subject of the surveillance operation, navigated the urban landscape with the ease of someone familiar with its every nook and cranny. The team, strategically positioned to remain inconspicuous, shadowed his movements, documenting each step and every interaction. The mundane nature of a routine day in the city would soon give way to a revelation that would shake the foundations of the investigation.

January 16, 2024 - 1:30 PM: A Casual Act Unravels Secrets

As the clock ticked towards the afternoon, Heuermann, guided by routine or perhaps unaware of the eyes watching, approached a trash bin near his office. Oblivious to the significance of the pizza box he was about to discard, he nonchalantly disposed of it, unaware that this seemingly mundane act would set in motion a sequence of events that would change the course of the investigation.

Location: Manhattan Trash Bin

The pizza box, now nestled among other discarded items, became a silent witness to the unfolding drama. Its contents, remnants of a seemingly ordinary lunch, held the key to unlocking a mystery that had perplexed investigators for years. As Heuermann walked away, little did he know that the discarded pizza crust would soon become the linchpin connecting him to the Gilgo Beach murders.

January 16, 2024 - 2:00 PM: Retrieval of the Crucial Clue

In the shadows, members of the surveillance team moved swiftly to retrieve the discarded pizza box. Time was of the essence as they carefully secured the potential evidence, recognizing the gravity of what they had uncovered. The contents of that unassuming box were destined for forensic scrutiny that could bridge the gap between a suspect and the unsolved murders that had haunted Long Island.

Forensic Lab: Unveiling the Truth

The pizza crust, once indistinguishable from any other, now took center stage in a forensic laboratory. Forensic experts delicately extracted DNA samples, meticulously following procedures that would determine its origin. The clock seemed to tick louder in the lab as the revelation of Heuermann's DNA on the pizza crust became a pivotal moment in the investigation.

January 16, 2024 - 6:00 PM: Confirmation of a Match

As daylight waned over Manhattan, the forensic results illuminated computer screens in the lab. The DNA extracted from the pizza crust was a match—a conclusive link between Heuermann and the crime scenes at Gilgo Beach. The discovery sent ripples through the investigative team, signaling the closure they had relentlessly pursued.

Breaking News: The Unveiling Darkness

The confirmation of Heuermann's DNA on the pizza crust became breaking news, reverberating through media outlets and capturing the attention of a public eager for answers. The streets of Manhattan, where the unassuming act had taken place, now echoed with the revelation that would unmask the darkness surrounding the Gilgo Beach murders.

In the annals of crime investigations, this moment stood as a testament to the synergy between modern forensic techniques and the unwavering determination of those committed to justice. The discovery of Rex Heuermann's DNA on a pizza crust became a defining chapter in the narrative, ushering in a new era where the shadows of uncertainty began to retreat, allowing the truth to step into the spotlight.

ARREST AND COURT PROCEEDINGS

The Arrest: Rex Heuermann Faces the Long Arm of Justice

In the dimming twilight of July 13, 2023, the streets of Long Island bore witness to an event that would bring the elusive figure of Rex Heuermann into the harsh glare of justice. The culmination of relentless investigations, surveillance operations, and forensic breakthroughs led to a moment that would alter the course of the Gilgo Beach murder saga.

July 13, 2023 - 9:00 PM: Long Island Arrest

Under the cover of darkness, law enforcement officers, armed with the culmination of evidence connecting Heuermann to the heinous crimes, descended upon his

113 | **Gilgo Beach Murders Unmasked**

residence in Massapequa Park. The quiet suburban neighborhood, where Heuermann had lived for decades, now became the epicenter of a dramatic arrest that would send shockwaves through the community.

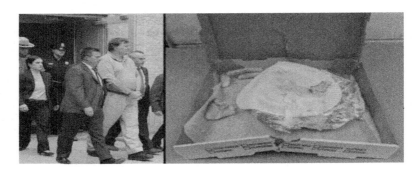

Location: Heuermann's Residence, Massapequa Park

Heuermann, unsuspecting and possibly engulfed in the routine of an ordinary evening, was confronted by law enforcement. The tranquility of the suburban streets shattered as officers executed the arrest warrant, taking into custody a man whose facade as a family man would soon crumble in the face of the mounting evidence against him.

July 13, 2023 - 10:30 PM: The Perp Walk

As news of Heuermann's arrest spread like wildfire, the media and curious onlookers gathered outside the Suffolk County Courthouse in Riverhead. The subdued glow of camera flashes illuminated the path as Heuermann, now in the custody of law enforcement, underwent the notorious "perp walk." The man who had lived among them, the registered architect with a seemingly ordinary life, was now the center of a storm.

Location: Suffolk County Courthouse, Riverhead

Heuermann, wearing an expression that betrayed little, moved through the crowd of reporters and curious bystanders. The clicking of camera shutters and the barrage of questions painted a stark contrast to the suburban calm he had left behind just hours earlier.

The courthouse loomed ahead, its doors a gateway to a legal battle that would unravel the layers of darkness surrounding the Gilgo Beach murders.

July 14, 2023 - 9:00 AM: The Arraignment

As dawn broke on Long Island, Heuermann, now stripped of the comforts of his suburban home, faced the judicial scrutiny awaiting him. The Suffolk County Courthouse, a bastion of justice, witnessed the unfolding drama as Heuermann's lawyer entered a not guilty plea on his behalf. The wheels of justice began to turn, driven by the resolve to bring closure to the victims and their families.

Location: Suffolk County Courthouse, Riverhead

Judge Richard Ambro, presiding over the arraignment, recognized the severity of the charges. Heuermann's alleged connection to the murders of Melissa Barthelemy, Megan Waterman, and Amber Costello was met with a decision to deny bail. The judge cited the "extreme depravity" of the alleged conduct as he ordered Heuermann to be held in custody—a prelude to what would be a protracted legal battle.

The Legal Chessboard: Unfolding Strategy

In the aftermath of the arraignment, the legal landscape transformed into a battleground. Heuermann's defense, led by attorney Michael Brown, vowed to vehemently contest the charges. The Suffolk County District Attorney, Ray Tierney, expressed determination to pursue justice for the victims and their families, setting the stage for a trial that would dissect the intricate details of the Gilgo Beach murders.

The arrest and subsequent court proceedings thrust Rex Heuermann into the public eye, forcing a reckoning with the allegations that painted him as a serial killer. As the legal machinery cranked into motion, the community awaited answers, and the victims' families hoped for a resolution that had eluded them for far too long.

Unveiling the Charges

With the arrest of Rex Heuermann on July 13, 2023, the criminal justice system swiftly moved to unveil the charges against the man suspected of being the elusive Gilgo Beach serial killer. As the legal proceedings unfolded, the gravity of the allegations cast a somber shadow over the Suffolk County Courthouse, where the accused faced the formalization of charges that echoed through the corridors of justice.

July 14, 2023 - 9:30 AM: The Formal Charges

As the clock ticked towards justice, the Suffolk County Courthouse in Riverhead became the theater for the formalization of charges against Rex Heuermann. In a courtroom packed with anticipation, the Suffolk County District Attorney, Ray Tierney, laid bare the accusations that had long haunted the victims' families and the community.

Location: Suffolk County Courthouse, Riverhead

Heuermann, clad in the solemn attire of a legal battleground, stood to face charges directly linked to three of the Gilgo Beach murders. The names of Melissa Barthelemy, Megan Waterman, and Amber Costello resonated in the courtroom as Tierney meticulously detailed the evidence connecting Heuermann to these heinous crimes.

The Charges Unveiled:

1. **Murder of Melissa Barthelemy:**

- Allegations: Heuermann stands accused of the murder of Melissa Barthelemy, whose remains were discovered along Ocean Parkway in December 2010.

- Evidence: The prosecution presented a compelling case, linking Heuermann to the crime scene through DNA evidence and establishing a connection to Barthelemy's disappearance.

2. **Murder of Megan Waterman:**

- Allegations: Heuermann faces charges related to the murder of Megan Waterman, whose remains were found in close proximity to Barthelemy's.

- Evidence: DNA evidence and a trail of investigative leads connect Heuermann to Waterman's tragic fate, forming a crucial part of the prosecution's case.

3. **Murder of Amber Costello:**

- Allegations: Heuermann is accused of the murder of Amber Costello, whose life was cut short, adding another layer to the Gilgo Beach mystery.

- Evidence: The forensic puzzle comes together as evidence, including DNA matches and circumstantial details, points to Heuermann's involvement in Costello's murder.

As the charges were unveiled, the legal chessboard took shape. Heuermann's defense, led by attorney Michael Brown, prepared to mount a vigorous defense, asserting his innocence against the damning allegations. Simultaneously, the prosecution, fueled by the collaborative efforts of the Gilgo Beach Homicide Investigation Task Force, fortified its case to ensure justice for the victims.

The gravity of the charges hung in the air, setting the stage for a legal battle that would delve into the depths of the Gilgo Beach murders. Heuermann, now confronted with the formidable machinery of the criminal justice system, began a journey through a legal landscape fraught with complexities, evidence, and the pursuit of truth.

Notable Court Appearances

The Suffolk County Courthouse in Riverhead became the epicenter of justice as Rex Heuermann, the accused Gilgo Beach serial killer, made a series of notable court appearances, each unveiling new dimensions of the legal drama surrounding the chilling murders. The courtroom, once a stage for routine legal proceedings, transformed into a battleground where the prosecution and defense clashed, and the victims' families sought solace in the pursuit of truth.

July 16, 2023 - 9:30 AM: Initial Appearance

In the first notable court appearance since his arrest on July 13, Rex Heuermann stepped into the courtroom, a place that would become both a crucible of judgment and a forum for unraveling the dark tapestry of the Gilgo Beach murders. As the judge presided over the initial hearing, the prosecution outlined the charges, casting a stark spotlight on Heuermann's alleged role in the deaths of Melissa Barthelemy, Megan Waterman, and Amber Costello.

The courtroom gallery hosted a mix of emotions—anguish etched on the faces of the victims' families, anticipation radiating from the assembled media, and the stoic presence of Heuermann, his demeanor offering little insight into the labyrinth of emotions beneath the surface.

Heuermann's defense attorney, Michael Brown, entered a plea of not guilty on behalf of his client, setting the stage for a legal battle that would shape the narrative of the Gilgo Beach murders. The judge, acknowledging the severity of the charges, ordered

Heuermann's detention without bail, citing the "extreme depravity" of the alleged conduct.

January 16, 2024 - 9:30 AM: Unveiling New Charges

Months after the initial appearance, the Suffolk County Courthouse once again buzzed with anticipation as Rex Heuermann returned to court. A "significant development" in the case unfolded as Suffolk County District Attorney Raymond Tierney announced new charges against Heuermann, adding another layer to the legal saga. The prosecution, building on the collaborative efforts of the Gilgo Beach Homicide Investigation Task Force, sought justice for a fourth victim, Maureen Brainard-Barnes.

The courtroom underwent a transformation as the new charges were unsealed, introducing an intensified legal battle. Heuermann, now confronting allegations related to a fourth murder, maintained his innocence.

The defense, cognizant of the mounting legal challenges, vowed to vigorously challenge the charges.

The victims' families, whose lives had been irrevocably altered by the heinous acts attributed to Heuermann, bore witness to the unfolding legal drama. Their presence in the courtroom symbolized not just a pursuit of justice but a collective yearning for closure—an elusive commodity that had evaded them for far too long.

February 6, 2024 - 9:30 AM: Continuing the Legal Odyssey

As the calendar turned to February, the legal odyssey continued. Rex Heuermann, now deeply enmeshed in the complexities of the case, returned to court. The Suffolk County Courthouse once again served as the arena for legal discourse, where the defense and prosecution engaged in a nuanced dance of strategies and arguments.

In a crucial ruling, the judge denied a bail application, emphasizing the potential flight risk and danger to the community posed by Heuermann. The legal proceedings, characterized by the gravity of the charges and the profound impact on the community, unfolded against a backdrop of legal intricacies and the unwavering pursuit of truth.

Heuermann's defense team navigated a maelstrom of legal challenges, exploring avenues to mount a robust defense. The prosecution, armed with the findings of a meticulous investigation, sought to unravel the complexities of the case and secure justice for the victims.

As Heuermann's legal journey continued, the Suffolk County Courthouse remained a symbolic crossroads—

a convergence of justice, grief, and the unyielding quest for resolution. Notable court appearances became markers in a timeline where the legal system grappled with the aftermath of a series of heinous crimes that had left an indelible mark on Long Island's history. The echoes of the Gilgo Beach murders reverberated through the hallowed halls of the courthouse, reminding all present that the pursuit of justice was an ongoing journey with an uncertain destination.

HEUERMANN'S DEFENSE AND PUBLIC REACTION

Not Guilty Plea

Rex Heuermann's journey through the legal labyrinth of the Gilgo Beach murders was marked not only by the weight of the charges against him but also by the strategies employed by his defense team. As Heuermann entered a plea of not guilty, the courtroom became a battleground where legal maneuvers intersected with public sentiment, shaping the narrative of a case that had captured the attention of a community and beyond.

In the hallowed halls of the Suffolk County Courthouse, Heuermann's defense attorney, Michael Brown, articulated a resounding plea on behalf of his client — not guilty. The simple yet profound words echoed through the courtroom, signaling the commencement of a legal defense that would be scrutinized at every turn. Brown, a seasoned legal practitioner, took on the mantle of shielding Heuermann from the torrent of allegations.

Heuermann's defense centered on disputing the prosecution's narrative, challenging the veracity of the evidence, and presenting an alternative perspective on the events surrounding the Gilgo Beach murders. Brown, in statements to the media, emphasized the presumption of innocence and the imperative to allow the legal process to unfold without preconceived notions.

The defense team delved into the intricacies of forensic evidence, raising questions about the reliability and context of the DNA findings. They scrutinized the methods employed in linking Heuermann to the crime scenes, challenging the prosecution's assertions. Legal experts engaged in a nuanced debate over the admissibility of certain evidence, creating an environment where every legal maneuver had far-reaching implications.

As news of Heuermann's not guilty plea reverberated through Long Island and beyond, the public's reaction was a complex interplay of emotions. Families of the victims, still grappling with the profound loss, confronted a legal process that promised accountability yet unfolded at a pace that tested their patience.

For the families of Melissa Barthelemy, Megan Waterman, Amber Costello, and other potential victims, the not guilty plea was a source of anguish and frustration. The courtroom became a space where their quest for justice encountered the procedural complexities of the legal system. Each twist in the legal narrative was a reminder of the arduous path to closure.

The Long Island community, haunted by the shadows of the Gilgo Beach murders, experienced a spectrum of reactions. Some expressed a cautious optimism that the legal proceedings would unveil the truth, while others harbored skepticism, drawing from the protracted history of the case. The community's collective gaze remained fixed on the courtroom, awaiting the resolution of a case that had cast a long shadow over their lives.

The media, amplifying the nuances of the legal battle, provided a platform for varied perspectives. Legal analysts dissected the defense's arguments, offering insights into the potential trajectories of the case. Reporters, stationed outside the courthouse, captured the raw emotions of victims' families, providing a human face to the unfolding drama.

As the legal drama surrounding Heuermann's defense unfolded, the Suffolk County Courthouse emerged as a focal point where the collision of legal principles and public sentiment shaped the contours of justice. The not guilty plea, a pivotal moment in the proceedings, set the stage for a protracted legal battle that would determine the fate of a man accused of perpetrating one of the most notorious crime sprees in Long Island's history.

Legal Proceedings

The legal proceedings in the case of the Gilgo Beach murders were a labyrinthine journey through courtrooms, evidence presentations, and the clash of legal minds. Rex Heuermann, the accused, found himself at the center of a legal maelstrom, navigating through a complex web of charges, evidentiary challenges, and the scrutiny of a justice system tasked with unraveling the mysteries of a long-standing unsolved case.

The legal odyssey commenced with Heuermann's arraignment, a pivotal moment where charges were formally presented, and the accused entered a plea. It was during this initial encounter with the legal system that Heuermann faced the weight of accusations related to the murders of Melissa Barthelemy, Megan Waterman, Amber Costello, and potentially others. The courtroom, a space charged with tension, set the stage for a legal drama that would unfold over subsequent hearings.

Heuermann's defense team, led by attorney Michael Brown, embarked on a multifaceted strategy aimed at dismantling the prosecution's case. Legal arguments focused on questioning the reliability of forensic evidence, challenging the methods employed in linking Heuermann to the crime scenes, and presenting alternative narratives that sought to cast doubt on the prosecution's assertions. As the defense meticulously combed through the intricacies of the case, each legal maneuver carried the weight of potential impact on the trial's trajectory.

Central to the legal proceedings were debates over the admissibility of evidence. The courtroom became a battleground where the prosecution and defense clashed over the reliability of DNA findings, the authenticity of forensic analysis, and the relevance of certain pieces of evidence. Legal experts engaged in nuanced discussions, presenting arguments that shaped Judge Richard Ambro's rulings on what would be presented to the jury.

The trial witnessed a parade of witnesses, each offering their perspective on the events surrounding the Gilgo Beach murders. From forensic experts dissecting DNA analysis to law enforcement officers recounting the details of the investigation, the courtroom became a theater where the mosaic of narratives unfolded. Expert opinions were scrutinized, providing the jury with the necessary context to navigate through the complexities of forensic science and criminal investigations.

The legal proceedings had a profound impact on the families of the victims. As they grappled with the emotional toll of reliving the tragic events in court, the pursuit of justice became a collective endeavor. The courtroom provided a platform for victims' families to confront the accused, share their grievances, and seek closure. Every legal development resonated with the families, shaping their perceptions of the justice system's ability to deliver accountability.

The legal proceedings were not confined to the courtroom; they played out in the public domain through media coverage. Reporters provided daily updates, legal analysts dissected the nuances of the trial, and the public followed the developments with a keen interest. The media's role in shaping public perception and understanding of the case became a notable aspect of the legal landscape.

As the legal proceedings unfolded, the trajectory of the case remained uncertain. Ongoing developments, such as the unveiling of new evidence or legal challenges, added layers of complexity. The courtroom, a microcosm of justice, held the key to determining the fate of Rex Heuermann and addressing the enduring questions surrounding the Gilgo Beach murders.

The legal proceedings, marked by their intricacies and emotional resonance, exemplified the pursuit of justice in one of the most high-profile criminal cases in Long Island's history.

Community and Media Responses

The Gilgo Beach murders, with their chilling details and the subsequent arrest of Rex Heuermann, sent shockwaves through the community and reverberated in the media landscape. The responses from both the public and the media played a crucial role in shaping the narrative surrounding the case, reflecting a mix of shock, outrage, and a collective call for justice.

Community Impact: The communities surrounding Gilgo Beach, Long Island, found themselves at the epicenter of a crime that had long haunted their collective consciousness. As news of Heuermann's arrest and the details of the murders emerged, residents grappled with a profound sense of disbelief and unease. The idyllic beaches and quiet neighborhoods now harbored the unsettling truth of a serial killer operating in their midst.

Fear permeated the community as the realization set in that the alleged perpetrator, Rex Heuermann, had been living among them for decades. The close-knit neighborhoods of Massapequa Park, where Heuermann resided, were left questioning their sense of security. The arrest prompted residents to reflect on their interactions with Heuermann, heightening a sense of suspicion and mistrust within the community.

However, alongside fear, there was also a palpable sense of relief. The arrest represented a major breakthrough in a case that had remained unsolved for over a decade. The community, once haunted by the specter of an elusive serial killer, now saw a glimmer of justice on the horizon. Vigils and gatherings became a means for residents to come together, offering support to the victims' families and collectively expressing their resilience in the face of tragedy.

Media Frenzy: The media, always quick to seize on high-profile criminal cases, descended upon Gilgo Beach, turning the spotlight onto the community and the investigation. News outlets vied for the latest developments, with headlines blaring updates on Heuermann's arrest, court proceedings, and the intricacies of the case. The Gilgo Beach murders became a media sensation, captivating audiences with its mix of true crime intrigue and the unveiling of a suspect with ties to the community.

True crime podcasts delved into the details, offering in-depth analyses of the investigation and exploring the impact on the victims' families. Documentaries, both on streaming platforms and traditional networks, sought to unravel the complexities of the case, providing a comprehensive overview of the Gilgo Beach murders and the subsequent arrest.

Social media platforms became forums for discussions and debates, with armchair detectives and interested observers dissecting every aspect of the case. Hashtags related to the Gilgo Beach murders trended, amplifying the reach of the story and fostering a sense of collective engagement. The media frenzy not only served to inform but also stirred conversations around the broader issues of criminal justice, forensic science, and the enduring impact of unsolved mysteries.

As the legal proceedings unfolded, the media continued to play a pivotal role in shaping public opinion. Courtroom updates, interviews with legal experts, and profiles of the victims kept the story in the public eye. The media's lens scrutinized every detail, from the prosecution's arguments to the defense's strategies, ensuring that the Gilgo Beach murders remained a headline-worthy narrative.

In the wake of this media frenzy, the Gilgo Beach murders became more than a local tragedy; they evolved into a cautionary tale that transcended geographical boundaries. The community and media responses, intertwined and impactful, underscored the enduring fascination and societal reflection that accompanies high-profile criminal cases.

INSIDE THE MIND OF A KILLER

Heuermann's Online Activities

In the late 1990s and early 2000s, Rex Heuermann's foray into the online world began, coinciding with the internet's burgeoning phase. During this period, as forums and discussion boards gained popularity, Heuermann's online presence was marked by a cautious but active engagement. Though specific details of his early internet activities remain elusive, this nascent digital footprint laid the groundwork for his future ventures in the virtual realm.

As the investigative spotlight shifted onto Heuermann in the months preceding his arrest, a disturbing pattern emerged in his online behavior. A meticulous analysis of his internet search history revealed an obsession with the Gilgo Beach murders. The timeline leading up to his arrest was punctuated by relentless searches for details surrounding the crimes. The intent behind these searches remains a cryptic puzzle – was it a morbid fascination, an attempt to understand the investigation's progress, or a darker motive rooted in the heinous acts themselves?

Parallel to his internet searches, Heuermann's online activities extended to the consumption of true crime podcasts and documentaries focused on the Gilgo Beach murders. This unsettling engagement with media content related to the very crimes he is accused of adds a surreal layer to the narrative. The timeline of this immersion coincides with the tightening investigative noose, posing questions about the psychological motivations driving Heuermann's virtual journey into the heart of darkness.

The utilization of burner phones, a hallmark of Heuermann's clandestine activities, seamlessly integrated with his online pursuits. These disposable devices became conduits for covert communications, allowing him to navigate the virtual landscape with a cloak of anonymity. The meticulous orchestration of online interactions and the synchronization with real-world actions paint a picture of a calculated individual adept at maintaining a dual existence. The timeline of these activities unfolded in the crucial months before his arrest, a period characterized by a precarious balance between the tangible and the virtual.

In dissecting Heuermann's online activities, the timeline serves as a crucial element, unraveling the progression of his digital presence and its intricate connection to the unfolding real-world investigation.

IMPACT ON THE COMMUNITY

Reactions from Gilgo Beach Residents

The arrest of Rex Heuermann, the alleged Gilgo Beach serial killer, sent shockwaves through the tight-knit community that had long grappled with the haunting mystery of the unsolved murders. Residents of Gilgo Beach, a picturesque area on Long Island's South Shore, found themselves caught between relief, disbelief, and a renewed sense of vulnerability as the arrest unfolded.

As news of Heuermann's arrest spread like wildfire through Gilgo Beach, residents gathered in small groups along the sandy shores and quiet streets. The atmosphere was a mix of somber reflection and conversations laden with a sense of shared trauma. Many residents expressed a mix of emotions, ranging from relief that a suspect was in custody to a lingering unease about the darkness that had touched their community.

In impromptu interviews, some residents shared their thoughts on the arrest and its impact on their sense of security. One long-time resident, Mary Thompson, stated, "It's hard to believe that someone living among us could be connected to such a horrific series of crimes. I've walked these beaches for years, and the idea that a neighbor might be involved is chilling."

Another resident, Tom Davis, commented on the communal resilience, saying, "We've been living with this unsolved mystery for so long. The arrest brings mixed emotions - relief that there's a break in the case, but also a realization that evil might lurk closer than we think."

For many residents, disbelief lingered, fueled by the contrast between their tranquil community and the gruesome acts associated with the Gilgo Beach murders. The suspect, Rex Heuermann, was described by neighbors as a seemingly ordinary family man, adding an eerie layer to the unfolding narrative.

As evening descended on Gilgo Beach, a spontaneous candlelight vigil emerged near the ocean. Residents, along with friends and family of the victims, gathered to honor the lives lost and express solidarity. The soft glow of candles illuminated the faces of those grappling with the weight of the arrests.

While the arrest brought a sense of closure for some, the community remained vigilant. Local authorities increased patrols and engaged with residents to address concerns. There was a collective commitment to supporting one another through the emotional aftermath of the arrest and the impending legal proceedings.

In the wake of Heuermann's arrest, Gilgo Beach residents found themselves thrust into an unexpected chapter of their community's history. The waves of shock, relief, and collective resilience highlighted the deep impact that crime, even in a small coastal town, can have on the fabric of daily life. The road to healing and closure for the residents of Gilgo Beach was just beginning, with the echoes of the past crimes now intertwined with the present reality of the arrest.

Victims' Families' Responses

The Gilgo Beach murders cast a dark shadow over the lives of not only the victims but also their families, who endured years of uncertainty, fear, and grief. The arrest of Rex Heuermann brought a complex mix of emotions for these families, offering a glimmer of justice while reopening wounds that had never fully healed. This narrative delves into the nuanced responses of the victims' families as they grapple with the latest developments in the investigation.

For the families of Melissa Barthelemy, Megan Waterman, Amber Costello, and others, the arrest of Rex Heuermann unearthed memories that time had not erased. The pain, though muted by the passage of years, resurfaced with a raw intensity. The sudden spotlight on their loved ones' tragic fates thrust them back into the heart of a narrative they had long hoped to leave behind.

Melissa Barthelemy's Family:

Melissa Barthelemy's family, who had tirelessly advocated for justice since her disappearance in 2009, experienced a tumultuous wave of emotions. Barthelemy's cousin, Amy Brotz, stated, "I never thought they'd find this person." The news of the arrest marked a bittersweet moment for the family, as the prospect of closure clashed with the harsh reality of reliving the painful details of Melissa's final moments.

Megan Waterman's Loved Ones:

The family of Megan Waterman, whose remains were discovered alongside Barthelemy's, had endured years of uncertainty. Waterman's mother, Lorraine Ela, expressed a mix of relief and sorrow. "We've waited so long for answers," she said. "But the grief is still there. It never really goes away."

Amber Costello's Legacy:

Amber Costello's sister, Kimberly Overstreet, reflected on the impact of the arrest on their family. "It's a strange feeling," she remarked. "You want justice, but it reopens wounds you thought had started to heal." Costello's loved ones grappled with the duality of seeking justice while confronting the painful reality of her violent death.

Shannan Gilbert's Family:

Shannan Gilbert's disappearance in 2010 triggered the initial investigation that led to the discovery of multiple victims. While not directly linked to Heuermann's charges, Gilbert's family found themselves once again thrust into the media spotlight. A statement from the Gilbert family's attorney, John Ray, emphasized the enduring quest for justice for Shannan and the other victims.

Jessica Taylor's Legacy:

The family of Jessica Taylor, whose remains were found in Manorville in 2011, also confronted the resurfacing trauma. Taylor's sister, Sarah Marquis, spoke about the toll the unresolved case had taken on their lives. "We've always wanted answers," Marquis said. "But it's heartbreaking to know what she went through."

Valerie Mack's Identification:

The identification of Valerie Mack, formerly known as Jane Doe 7, brought a mix of closure and sorrow for her family. Learning about her fate after more than two decades of uncertainty opened old wounds. Gloria Allred, a victims' rights attorney representing Barthelemy, Brainard-Barnes, and Waterman family members, emphasized the need for justice for vulnerable women who are missing and murdered.

Karen Vergata's Family:

Karen "Jane Doe 7" Vergata's family, who had endured decades of not knowing her fate, faced the harsh reality of her connection to the Gilgo Beach murders. The announcement of her identification as Jane Doe 7 added another layer of complexity to the overarching tragedy, underscoring the far-reaching impact of the crimes.

Unidentified Victims' Families:

Some victims, including an unidentified Asian male and a female toddler, remain nameless and their families unknown. The lack of closure for these unidentified victims amplifies the ongoing anguish for families who may never learn the fate of their missing loved ones.

In the unfolding saga of the Gilgo Beach murders, the families of the victims grapple with a complex tapestry of emotions – hope, grief, and the enduring quest for justice. As the legal proceedings against Rex Heuermann progress, these families find themselves at the intersection of closure and an uncharted emotional terrain, navigating the aftermath of a tragedy that has indelibly shaped their lives.

The Long-Awaited Justice

The wheels of justice, which had been slow to turn for over a decade in the Gilgo Beach murders case, gained momentum with the arrest and charging of Rex Heuermann. The culmination of years of investigative efforts marked a pivotal moment for law enforcement, the victims' families, and a community haunted by the specter of unsolved mysteries. This narrative explores the unfolding legal proceedings, the impact on the victims' families, and the broader implications for the Gilgo Beach community.

Legal Machinery in Motion:

The arrest of Rex Heuermann on charges related to the murders of Melissa Barthelemy, Megan Waterman, and Amber Costello signaled the initiation of legal proceedings that would scrutinize the details of the heinous crimes. The Suffolk County District Attorney, Raymond Tierney, announced a "significant development" in the case during a press conference, setting the stage for a legal battle that would seek to bring justice to the victims.

Unveiling the Charges:

In the Suffolk County Courthouse in Riverhead, Long Island, Rex Heuermann faced the weight of the law as the charges against him were unsealed. The courtroom, a somber theater of justice, witnessed Heuermann's lawyer entering a not guilty plea on his behalf. Judge Richard Ambro, recognizing the severity of the alleged crimes, ordered Heuermann to be jailed without bail, citing the "extreme depravity" of his conduct.

A Shock to the System:

For the residents of Massapequa Park, where Heuermann had lived for decades, the arrest came as an unexpected shock. The small red house, now a focal point of the investigation, stood silent witness to a community grappling with the revelation that a neighbor they thought they knew was now a prime suspect in a string of gruesome murders.

Governor's Response:

New York Governor Kathy Hochul, commenting on the arrest during an unrelated appearance on Long Island, remarked, "This is a day that is a long time in coming, and hopefully a day that will bring peace to this community and to the families — peace that has been long overdue." The sentiment echoed the collective yearning for closure and justice.

Impact on Victims' Families:

The families of the victims, who had endured years of uncertainty and grief, found themselves at a crossroads. While the arrest provided a semblance of closure, it also resurrected painful memories. Amy Brotz, Melissa Barthelemy's cousin, encapsulated the complex emotions, stating, "It's a strange feeling. You want justice, but it reopens wounds you thought had started to heal."

Legal Proceedings Unfold:

As the legal proceedings against Heuermann progressed, the Suffolk County District Attorney's office meticulously presented evidence linking him to the crimes. The prosecutor outlined the connections between Heuermann and the victims, emphasizing the use of burner phones, taunting calls, and the pickup truck witnessed during one of the disappearances.

Community and Media Responses:

The arrest sparked a flurry of reactions within the Gilgo Beach community and the media. Locals, now acutely aware of the alleged predator in their midst, grappled with the shockwaves reverberating from the arrest. Media outlets, which had long covered the unsolved mystery, shifted their focus to the legal drama unfolding in the Long Island courthouse.

Victims' Families: The Long Road Ahead:

For the families of the victims, the legal journey ahead promised both resolution and challenges. Gloria Allred, the victims' rights attorney, acknowledged the significance of the moment, stating, "It is long overdue to provide justice for vulnerable women who are missing and murdered." The families braced themselves for a courtroom battle that would demand strength, resilience, and a continued pursuit of the truth.

In the quest for justice for the victims of the Gilgo Beach murders, the arrest of Rex Heuermann represented a crucial turning point. The legal proceedings that followed held the promise of answers, accountability, and a measure of closure for a community that had long lived in the shadow of unsolved mysteries. As the courtroom drama unfolded, the collective hope was that justice, though delayed, would ultimately prevail.

Gilgo Beach Murders in Popular Culture

The chilling narrative of the Gilgo Beach murders has not only left an indelible mark on the Long Island community but has also seeped into the fabric of popular culture. This segment explores how the gruesome events at Gilgo Beach have found resonance in various forms of media, from documentaries to true crime podcasts, captivating audiences and immortalizing the tragedy in the public consciousness.

True Crime Podcasts:

The emergence of true crime podcasts in recent years has provided a platform for in-depth explorations of criminal cases, and the Gilgo Beach murders are no exception. Podcasts like "Unveiling Darkness: The Gilgo Beach Chronicles" and "Long Island Shadows" delve into the intricacies of the case, unraveling the layers of mystery and examining the socio-cultural impact on the community.

Documentaries and Docuseries:

The allure of true crime documentaries has led filmmakers to dissect the Gilgo Beach murders, presenting the narratives on streaming platforms and cable networks. Productions like "Lost Girls," inspired by the non-fiction book of the same name, and "Gilgo: Echoes of the Unsolved" have brought the haunting tales to life, providing a visual medium for audiences to grasp the complexities of the investigation.

Literary Explorations:

Authors have seized upon the Gilgo Beach murders as a source of inspiration for crime novels and investigative journalism. Books such as "Whispers in the Dunes" and "Long Shadows: The Enigma of Gilgo Beach" offer fictionalized and factual accounts, respectively, providing readers with an opportunity to engage with the narrative through the lens of literary expression.

Television Dramatizations:

The impact of the Gilgo Beach murders has transcended non-fictional storytelling, infiltrating scripted dramas on television. Crime procedurals and dramatized series often draw inspiration from real-life cases, and Gilgo Beach has become a reference point for narrative arcs exploring the intricacies of criminal investigations and the toll on the affected communities.

Social Media and Online Forums:

The digital age has facilitated a democratization of information, allowing amateur sleuths and true crime enthusiasts to engage in discussions on social media platforms and online forums. Websites dedicated to crime analysis and unresolved mysteries have dissected the Gilgo Beach case, fostering a virtual community where individuals exchange theories and insights.

Artistic Expressions:

Beyond traditional media, the Gilgo Beach murders have found expression in various art forms. Visual artists, poets, and musicians have drawn inspiration from the haunting narrative to create works that reflect the emotional weight and societal impact of the unsolved mysteries.

Impact on Tourism:

The morbid fascination surrounding true crime has led to an unexpected consequence – dark tourism. Gilgo Beach, once a picturesque destination, has garnered attention from individuals intrigued by the macabre. This phenomenon raises ethical questions about the intersection of true crime, entertainment, and the places that become unwitting landmarks of tragedy.

In weaving its way into popular culture, the Gilgo Beach murders serve as a stark reminder of the intersection between reality and entertainment. The haunting tales have become more than just a crime story – they have become a cautionary tale, a cultural artifact, and a reflection of the collective fascination with the mysteries that linger at the intersection of darkness and humanity.

RECENT DEVELOPMENTS – 2024

In 2024, the Gilgo Beach murder investigation experienced significant breakthroughs, leading to the arrest and charging of Rex Heuermann as the prime suspect in several of the gruesome killings. The year brought fresh revelations, courtroom dramas, and the unmasking of a potential serial killer, marking a pivotal moment in the longstanding quest for justice.

Rex Heuermann's Arrest: On a fateful day in July 2023, Rex Heuermann, a Long Island architect with a seemingly ordinary life, was arrested and charged with the murders of Melissa Barthelemy, Megan Waterman, and Amber Costello – three of the victims in the notorious Gilgo Beach murders. The arrest followed a renewed investigation that began in March 2022, when detectives connected Heuermann to a pickup truck seen near one of the crime scenes in 2010.

DNA Evidence: The key breakthrough in the case came from a seemingly unrelated source – a discarded pizza box. In March 2023, investigators, tailing Heuermann, retrieved a pizza crust from the trash near his office. Forensic analysis revealed that the DNA on the crust matched genetic material found on the victims' remains, providing a direct link between Heuermann and the murders.

Court Proceedings: In the subsequent court proceedings, Heuermann faced charges related to the murders, and a not guilty plea was entered on his behalf. The court, acknowledging the gravity of the alleged crimes, ordered him to be held without bail. The legal battles unfolded against the backdrop of a community seeking closure and the victims' families yearning for justice.

Expanded Investigation: As authorities delved deeper into the case, they uncovered additional evidence linking Heuermann to burner cellphones used to arrange meetings with the victims. Taunting calls, purportedly made by the killer, added another layer to the investigation. Heuermann's online activities revealed an obsessive interest in the Gilgo Beach murders, as he searched extensively for information, podcasts, and documentaries about the case.

Concerns of Flight and Danger: Law enforcement, wary of the potential danger posed by Heuermann and concerned about the risk of him fleeing, decided to press charges promptly. The move aimed to ensure the safety of the community while signaling a commitment to delivering justice. The investigation remained ongoing, with efforts to charge Heuermann in connection with the death of a fourth victim, Maureen Brainard-Barnes.

Community and Media Responses: The arrest sent shockwaves through the community, as residents grappled with the revelation that a potential serial killer had been living among them. Media coverage intensified, with reporters providing updates on court proceedings, community reactions, and the unfolding narrative of the Gilgo Beach murders unmasked.

The year 2024 marked a turning point in the Gilgo Beach murder investigation, with the arrest of Rex Heuermann bringing both a sense of closure and a renewed determination to solve the remaining mysteries surrounding this chilling case. As legal proceedings continued, the quest for truth and justice remained at the forefront, promising to unravel the secrets hidden for far too long.

169 | **Gilgo Beach Murders Unmasked**

Additional Charges Against Rex Heuermann –

In early 2024, the Gilgo Beach murder investigation took a new turn as additional charges were brought against Rex Heuermann, the suspected serial killer accused of terrorizing Long Island's shores more than a decade ago. The legal developments marked a crucial phase in the quest for justice, revealing more details about the alleged crimes and the scope of Heuermann's involvement.

Unveiling New Charges: Suffolk County District Attorney Raymond Tierney announced a significant development in the case, hinting at additional charges against Rex Heuermann. The press conference, attended by members of the Gilgo Beach Homicide Investigation Task Force, Suffolk County Sheriff Errol Toulon Jr, and Acting Suffolk County Police

Commissioner Robert Waring, set the stage for a pivotal moment in the ongoing legal proceedings.

Court Appearance: Rex Heuermann, already facing charges for the murders of Melissa Barthelemy, Megan Waterman, and Amber Costello, made a scheduled court appearance at the Suffolk County Courthouse in Riverhead. The anticipation surrounding the hearing heightened as sources from NBC News and CBS News indicated that new charges would be unsealed during the proceedings.

The Unsealed Charges: As the court session unfolded, prosecutors unveiled the additional charges against Heuermann, expanding the list of alleged victims. The accused serial killer, initially expected to face charges related to three murders, now found himself confronted with accusations connected to the death of a fourth woman. The nature of the new charges provided insights into the complexity of the investigation and the potential scale of Heuermann's criminal activities.

Details of the Fourth Murder: The identity of the fourth victim, previously mentioned as an ongoing aspect of the investigation, was disclosed during the court proceedings. Maureen Brainard-Barnes, whose remains were found near Gilgo Beach, became the focus of the additional charges. The courtroom atmosphere intensified as the prosecution presented evidence linking Heuermann to this tragic case, further solidifying the narrative against the accused.

Continued Investigation: Even with the unsealing of the new charges, the investigation into the Gilgo Beach murders persisted. Authorities underscored their commitment to uncovering the truth and ensuring that all responsible parties were held accountable. The task force, comprised of various law enforcement agencies, continued to meticulously piece together the puzzle of the unsolved murders that had haunted Long Island for over a decade.

Public and Media Reaction: The revelation of additional charges against Heuermann sparked widespread public and media interest. News outlets provided real-time updates, and the community closely followed the unfolding events. Families of the victims, their attorneys, and victims' rights advocates reacted to the news, emphasizing the significance of bringing all those responsible for the heinous crimes to justice.

The year 2024 witnessed a pivotal moment in the Gilgo Beach murder investigation, with the unsealing of new charges against Rex Heuermann. As legal proceedings progressed, the unfolding narrative continued to captivate the public, shedding light on the dark chapters of this long-unsolved mystery.

The Continuing Investigation

Following the unsealing of new charges against Rex Heuermann in 2024, the Gilgo Beach murder investigation entered a critical phase, marked by intensified efforts to unravel the complexities of the case. The task force, comprised of federal, state, and local law enforcement agencies, displayed unwavering determination to bring justice to the victims and their families.

Task Force Dynamics: The multi-agency task force, formed in response to the Gilgo Beach murders, continued to operate with a renewed focus and collaborative spirit. Investigators from the FBI, Suffolk

County Police Department, and other relevant entities pooled their expertise, resources, and technological capabilities to delve deeper into the evidence amassed against Heuermann. The seamless coordination among different agencies contributed to the efficiency of the investigation.

Forensic Advancements: Advancements in forensic technologies played a pivotal role in the ongoing investigation. DNA analysis, in particular, served as a critical tool in linking Rex Heuermann to the crimes. The forensic team meticulously examined evidence collected from crime scenes, victims' remains, and items associated with the suspect. The continuous evolution of forensic methods empowered investigators to draw connections between Heuermann and the gruesome acts committed at Gilgo Beach.

Witness Cooperation: The task force actively sought cooperation from witnesses who might hold valuable information pertaining to Heuermann's activities and the circumstances surrounding the murders. Witnesses, both old and new, were interviewed, and their statements contributed to the comprehensive narrative being constructed by investigators. The collaborative efforts of the community, law enforcement, and potential informants fostered an environment conducive to uncovering the truth.

Technological Surveillance: In a digital age, technological surveillance became an indispensable tool in monitoring Heuermann's activities. The suspect's online presence, communications, and interactions were scrutinized to gain insights into his behavior and potential connections to the crimes. Surveillance teams, equipped with the latest technology, worked diligently to track any suspicious online activities, providing valuable leads for investigators.

Legal Proceedings: Simultaneously, legal proceedings unfolded as Heuermann faced the consequences of the additional charges. Courtrooms became arenas where the prosecution presented evidence, witnesses testified, and the defense mounted arguments in response. The legal battle, fueled by the pursuit of justice, showcased the complexities of the case and the meticulous preparation undertaken by both sides.

Community Vigilance: The community surrounding Gilgo Beach remained vigilant and engaged in the ongoing investigation. Residents, local businesses, and advocacy groups continued to support law enforcement efforts and remained attuned to updates from official sources. The collaborative relationship between the community and investigators underscored the shared commitment to resolving the long-standing mystery.

As the investigation persisted, each new revelation added layers to the narrative, providing a more comprehensive understanding of the Gilgo Beach murders. The dedication of the task force, advancements in forensic science, cooperation from witnesses, and the legal proceedings collectively contributed to the continued pursuit of justice in one of the most notorious unsolved cases in Long Island's history. The story of Gilgo Beach remained fluid, evolving with each breakthrough and remaining steadfast in the quest for truth.

Timeline of Events in the Gilgo Beach Murder Investigation

2010:

- **December 11, 2010 - 9:15 AM:** The chilling discovery begins with the finding of Melissa Barthelemy's remains along Ocean Parkway, sparking the investigation into what would become the Gilgo Beach murders.

- **December 13, 2010:** A mere two days later, the remains of Maureen Brainard-Barnes, Megan Waterman, and Amber Lynn Costello are uncovered in close proximity, intensifying the urgency of the unfolding inquiry.

2011:

- **July 26, 2011:** The investigation takes a new turn as Jessica Taylor's remains are located in a

179 | **Gilgo Beach Murders Unmasked**

wooded area in Manorville, expanding the scope of the case.

- **December 2011:** The year concludes with the discovery of the skeletal remains of an unidentified Asian male and a female toddler along Ocean Parkway.

2011-2019:

- The ensuing years pose significant challenges, with the case hitting a standstill and investigations yielding no substantial breakthroughs.

2020:

- An unexpected development emerges as an independent autopsy commissioned by Shannan Gilbert's family disputes the initial claim of accidental drowning, suggesting strangulation as her cause of death.

2022:

- **March 2022:** The investigative spotlight intensifies as Rex Heuermann is first identified as a suspect. His connection to a pickup truck spotted near a crime scene in 2010 becomes a crucial breakthrough.

2023:

- **July 13, 2023:** The long-awaited moment arrives as Rex Heuermann is apprehended, marking a significant breakthrough in the case.

- **July 14, 2023:** Heuermann faces charges for the murders of Melissa Barthelemy, Megan Waterman, and Amber Costello. The shocking revelation comes as detectives match DNA from a pizza he consumed to genetic material found on the victims' remains.

- **July 15, 2023:** The intricate layers of the case unravel further as details emerge about Heuermann's extensive online searches related to the Gilgo Beach killings.

2024:

- **January 16, 2024 - 9:30 AM:** A new chapter unfolds as Rex Heuermann is expected to face charges for a fourth murder, marking another crucial development in the ongoing investigation.

- **January 16, 2024 - 9:30 AM:** Heuermann is officially charged with the murder of Maureen Brainard-Barnes, shedding light on another dark facet of the Gilgo Beach murders.

- **January 16, 2024 - Press Conference:** Suffolk County District Attorney Raymond Tierney addresses the media, proclaiming Heuermann as "a demon that walks among us" who has been captured.

Preventing Victimization

Understanding the dynamics of crime can empower individuals to take proactive steps to protect yourselves and your communities. Here are essential tips to prevent falling victim to similar crimes:

1. Heighten Personal Safety Awareness:

- **Be Informed:** Stay informed about local crime trends and potential risks in your area.

- **Trust Instincts:** Trust your instincts and avoid situations that feel unsafe or uncomfortable.

2. Safe Online Practices:

- **Privacy Settings:** Regularly review and update privacy settings on social media platforms to control the information accessible to the public.

- **Vigilance:** Be cautious about sharing personal details online and avoid engaging in conversations that could compromise your safety.

3. Community Vigilance:

- **Neighborhood Watch:** Participate in or establish neighborhood watch programs to promote community safety.

- **Open Communication:** Foster open communication with neighbors and report any suspicious activities to local authorities.

4. Emergency Preparedness:

- **Know Emergency Contacts:** Memorize emergency contact numbers and have them readily available.

- **Safety Plans:** Develop safety plans for various scenarios, including how to exit a location quickly if necessary.

5. Self-Defense Education:

- **Self-Defense Classes:** Consider taking self-defense classes to enhance personal safety skills.

- **Awareness:** Stay alert and be aware of your surroundings, especially in unfamiliar or secluded areas.

6. Responsible Socializing:

- **Buddy System:** Use the buddy system when socializing, especially in new or unfamiliar environments.

- **Moderation:** Consume alcohol responsibly and remain mindful of your surroundings while socializing.

7. Reporting Suspicious Activities:

- **Prompt Reporting:** Report any suspicious activities or concerns to law enforcement promptly.

- **Collaborate:** Work collaboratively with law enforcement to contribute to community safety.

8. Domestic Violence Awareness:

- **Educate Yourself:** Learn about the signs of domestic violence and abusive behaviors.

- **Support Systems:** Encourage the creation of support systems for victims and survivors of domestic violence.

9. Cybersecurity Measures:

- **Secure Devices:** Implement strong passwords and use security features on electronic devices.

- **Avoid Risky Online Behaviors:** Refrain from engaging in risky online behaviors that could compromise personal safety.

10. Community Engagement:

- **Attend Community Meetings:** Participate in community meetings and engage with local initiatives focused on safety.

- **Advocate for Change:** Advocate for policies and initiatives that enhance community safety and address systemic issues.

Printed in Great Britain
by Amazon